THE NICE ENTREPRENEUR

HOW LEADING FROM THE HEART CAN MAKE ALL THE DIFFERENCE

BY BRIAN K. MONTGOMERY

Inspire On Purpose Publishing
Irving, Texas

The Nice Entrepreneur
How Leading from the Heart Can Make All the Difference

Copyright © 2016 Brian K. Montgomery

Inspire On Purpose Publishing
Irving, Texas
(888) 403-2727
http://inspireonpurpose.com
The Platform Publisher™

Printed in the United States of America

Library of Congress Control Number: 2016949137

ISBN-13: 978-1-941782-34-7

ACKNOWLEDGEMENTS

A special thank you to all the people who kept me motivated along the way to begin and finish this book, some of whom have no idea how vital a role they played. Every time I was ready to give up, one of you would call, email, or stop by to visit, motivating me to get back to it.

To my family, I hope I've made you proud. Maybe through this book, you'll learn a little something you didn't know before.

And thank you, Brenda, most of all for being my business partner, my wife, my friend, and the love of my life from the moment I saw you across that high school cafeteria. We've been through more than our fair share together, but I'm looking forward to enjoying every moment of life, part two, with you.

TABLE OF CONTENTS

PREFACE

A Maui Mystery

The stress began to melt away as soon as we left the runway. We'd waited a long time for this vacation. It was our joint birthday gift to each other in 2009.

We watched the Dallas skyline disappear and settled in for the long flight. Hours later, we looked out at the beautiful Hawaiian beaches as we landed in Maui.

It was more than I ever could have imagined and a far cry from the standard business trip I was accustomed to. We made sure to book the best of the best. From the moment Brenda and I checked in to the Four Seasons Resort, we received the finest first-class treatment.

The room itself was larger than life, with a bathroom as big as some houses I've been in. The marble floors, oversized bathtub, huge master-bath shower, gorgeous high ceilings, king-sized bed with luxurious fluffy pillows, and lush surroundings everywhere I looked, all screamed "five-star hotel."

When I walked out the back patio door of our room and stared at the beach, at the beautiful water, and felt the cool ocean breeze, I was stunned. This was beyond my wildest dreams.

Sitting with a hot cup of Kona coffee in hand, taking it all in, my mind began to wander. I asked myself the question that ultimately compelled me to write this book: Why me? Why am I here? Why do I get to enjoy this beautiful beach on this exotic island while so many other people will never leave their own backyards?

I'm nothing special. I was never voted "most likely to succeed," never made captain of the football team, and was never elected class officer. I once took an F in a speech class because I wouldn't get up in front of the class to talk. I didn't understand what equations such as $(X+1)/(Y+1)$ meant, and I struggled just to achieve a B average in high school. The highest level of education I completed was an associate's degree in a technical field. In fact, I made a C in the only business class I ever took.

How did I end up on an exclusive beach in Maui with the love of my life by my side? My name is Brian Montgomery, and I have a story to tell.

INTRODUCTION

Why It's Good to Remember Who You Are

If only I knew now what I knew then.

Read that again: If only I knew *now* what I knew *then*.

Yes, I know it's backwards from what you usually hear, so let me explain.

If you actually knew now what you knew then (or at least remembered what you'd learned throughout the years), where might you be today?

Most of us remember only a few key moments that define our lives and our value systems, yet every one of our decisions makes us who we are. That's why knowing *now* what you knew *then*, both the good and the bad, helps you understand who you are today.

My theory is if I know what got me here, and if I like where I am, I can continue making the right decisions, which will allow me to continue on my path. The sentiment expressed in the old adage "I wish I knew then what I know now" isn't controllable, but the sentiment expressed in "I wish I knew now what I knew then" is.

Take this knowledge and hold tight to the lessons you've learned, and then apply them to your future. Don't focus on the mistakes and failures in the past (that leads to regret), and don't focus on second thoughts. You can't change the past and you can't always control what happens. Use your past to help define a successful future.

This concept is the basis of my story. Look back and you'll realize a handful of truly memorable events impacted the way you turned out.

Of course, the easy ones to recall are the day you met your spouse, the day your children were born, and so on. If you haven't experienced these events yet, trust me, they will be days you remember.

But there are other events—sometimes smaller and seemingly insignificant at the time—in your personal and professional life that will have a lasting impact on your future. Those that stick with you also help define you.

Often those events come with strong emotions, and they may be positive or negative. Capturing and remembering those feelings can drive you to make decisions to experience those feelings again, or drive you to make decisions so that you never have to experience them again.

How do you define success? Maybe it's:

- a successful marriage with two kids and a dog,
- the corner office,
- a fancy car,

- a certain amount of money in the bank,
- friends you can count on no matter what,
- freedom to hike every national park in the nation, or
- time to go biking every weekend.

Everyone defines success differently. Whatever it looks like to you, I believe a set of common principles lead to and impact your success. Looking back at how I built my life and my company, it's clear every success I ever enjoyed resulted from applying four principles I believe are critical to living a successful life.

Growing up in a small town in southern Mississippi with very little money makes me appreciate everything I've accomplished. The simple values learned as a young person proved invaluable to me later in life:

- Learn everything you can.
- Be passionate about what you do.
- Have a vision for how to reach your goals, whatever they may be.
- Show integrity in everything you do.
- Be willing to step out there to accomplish your goals.

I'm going to share with you my story and experiences in hopes of helping you reach your success. As you read this book you'll discover how I applied four basic principles that took me far in life and in business. I hope they will be as helpful to you as they were to me, and that you, too, can use them to reach the success you dream of.

Principle 1: Learn It

Learning is fundamental to success. It begins the day you are born and continues throughout your lifetime. Learning to walk, learning to talk, and leaning to read and write are the earliest of learned activities. As we progress though childhood into adolescence and beyond, we learn additional skills that help us develop into who we will become.

Going to school, studying, and making good grades are just the beginning. Learning continues throughout your life as you apply your knowledge, experience, education, and most importantly your good character to the skills you learn and the opportunities you have.

Character is built over time and is the foundation of all you do. It's who you are and what you stand for. It defines the way you think, the way you act, your behavior, your overall personality, and your morality. What's more, it develops from past events. Who you are, the beliefs you hold, the convictions you carry – all these come from your life experiences. Your beliefs impact the way you respond or act, and your actions lead to the outcome.

Character means acting with integrity and treating others with respect. One of my favorite statements is, "To be respected, you must be willing to give it first." Respect is mutual. If you aren't willing to respect others, you will never receive it in return.

You are what you experience in life, modified by how you act on those experiences while guided by your value system.

You are the choices you make, and you will have many choices along your path. Choose to learn from each opportunity.

Principle 2: Love It

Ah, passion. The old saying, "Love what you do and you'll never work a day in your life" has definitely proven true for me.

I've signed millions of dollars of business in my career, but never considered myself a salesman. People who know me might argue that, but I believed in what I did and always sold from the heart. I never followed a formal presentation or created fancy handouts. In fact, I never made a sales presentation or ran a training class the same way twice.

My passion led to many changes in my career, helped me develop my vision and mission for my company, and ultimately resulted in great success. Passion was a driving factor behind most of the critical decisions I ever made.

If you want to make a change in your life, it begins with passion and attitude. From the moment you wake up and get out of bed, you'll be faced with decisions. Make the decision to have a good day and choose the corresponding attitude. Smiles beget smiles, and the opposite is just as true. You'll be presented with many opportunities to change your attitude, but don't let circumstances and other people dictate the choices you make.

I've heard many people say you can't be liked and also be respected, but I disagree. If you treat people with respect, even if you disagree with them, you actually can have both. Often in my career, people did things for me because they didn't want to let me down. I always knew that if I were liked and respected as a leader, I would receive the most out of others.

Even so, if I had to choose between being liked and being respected, I'd choose to be liked. That's just the way I am, and I make no apologies for it.

As you go through life, find your passion and then embrace it.

Principle 3: Live It

We've already talked about how your beliefs are part of your character and that your character provides your foundation. Now let's talk about putting that into play: stand behind what you believe and measure your decisions against your beliefs.

"Living it" is about putting your beliefs (and therefore, character) into practice. What's important to you? Do you believe in fairness? Live out fairness. Do you believe in integrity? Live with integrity. There are several character traits that I believe in strongly, but I'm going to highlight a few examples of how living those beliefs led to success in my career and life.

One of the most important character traits can also be one of the most difficult to learn: empathy. Stephen Covey describes it best in The 7 Habits of Highly Effective People when he talks about Habit 5, "Seek first to understand, then be understood."

Looking at situations from another person's point of view is one of the character traits I used most successfully in business. In every interaction, I asked questions such as, "Would I buy this?" "What would I think if I were told that?" "How would I react to that?"

Whether I was servicing equipment, selling services, hiring people, or training them, I always tried to look at the situation from the other person's point of view before trying to make my point or presentation.

I also believe strongly in having a servant mentality. This means asking "What can I do for you?" rather than "What's in it for me?" Unfortunately, when looking for a job, most people look for the company that pays the most or offers the best benefits. In other words, they look at potential employers and ask "What can you do for me?" The better approach would be to ask "What can I offer this company?"

By focusing on making your company successful and doing the absolute best job you can, you gain experience, build character, and advance your career. The money usually follows, but compensation comes in many forms. Experience and the relationships you develop can prove more valuable in the end. Sometimes people do dedicate time, energy, and passion to a company and aren't sufficiently compensated, but at the very least, they gain experience that can help them make better decisions in the future.

The decisions you make, the success you gain, the legacy you leave will all be directly determined by how you live your life. Know what's important and embody those traits in your decisions and behaviors.

Principle 4: Pursue It

Why was I the one on that beach?

I think it comes down to being willing to step out of my comfort zone, take a risk, and be willing to possibly lose everything for something I believed in.

Sometimes it's hard to imagine five, ten, fifteen, or thirty years down the road. It's easy to say you want to retire someday and travel the world, but what does that look like? Do you want to retire at age fifty? Do you want to visit twenty countries? How are you going to make that happen? You must know what you want out of life and then set the goals and objectives to achieve it.

Set goals and objectives. Write them down and review them regularly, at least once per year. If you don't know where to start, try the SMART Method (I'll tell you how I used it in Chapter 3).

Goals and objectives are vital to success. Goals are the "what" — what you want to achieve. Objectives are the "how" — how you are going to achieve that goal. It may well take many objectives to achieve your goals. What's more, your goals and objectives might change over time.

The road to success, however you define it, will have many twists and turns and perhaps some complete stops. Principles 1, 2, and 3 will help you get there, but there are many avenues to reach your destination. Some people take the direct route. Others like taking the scenic route. Some find themselves taking unexpected detours.

INTRODUCTION

If you want to be successful, no matter how you define it, you must be willing to do whatever it takes. If you don't play the game, you can't expect to win. In other words, if you want to win the lottery, you must buy a ticket.

Set your goal, then go out and pursue it.

We all have a story to tell. And this is my story.

If you knew your life would be chronicled in a book someday, what kind of book would it be? Would it be full of action and adventure? Would it be a mystery? A drama? A romance? A horror story? A tale of motivation?

Now what if everything you did in life were recounted in this book for others to read?

As far as I'm concerned, that's a pretty good reminder as you make daily decisions.

My bucket list has always included writing a book. Over the years, the type of book I've wanted to write has changed from fiction to nonfiction to biography to business. I finally decided that my story is worth telling, but only you can determine whether it's worth reading.

That's what this is — my life story. It relays the practical, common-sense approach that led me to build a wildly successful business by applying a few basic principles while dealing with life's opportunities and challenges. It chronicles how I took what I learned in my younger years and applied it to real life and my profession. It documents the challenges I faced, the opportunities I embraced, and the lessons I learned along the way. My success was due in large part to what I learned *not* to do as much as from what I learned *to* do.

Throughout my story, my actions continually express those four basic principles of success that impacted my life and career—learn it, love it, live it, and pursue it. I want to tell you how and where I learned these principles and how they helped me secure my life's goals. My story is meant to be inspirational and informative as I reveal how I overcame the inevitable obstacles that came my way by simply taking a commonsense, practical approach to business, treating people with compassion and doing the right thing, while striving to balance being respected with being liked.

It's easy to see how my outcomes have been a direct result of these four basic principles at work in my life. How you apply them—learn it, love it, live it, pursue it— will directly impact your life, too.

For those of you who have heard of the company I started, CREST Services, but never knew the story, perhaps this book will offer a different way to think about your company or serve as a guide to do business a bit differently.

For those who have never heard of me (or the company I built), I hope this book helps you realize that you can accomplish anything you set your mind to. The fact is, the situations you face, the challenges you confront, and above all the decisions you make affect everything in your life. These decisions point you in a direction, good or bad.

Regardless of what led you to this book and no matter what you gain from reading it, I actually wrote it both for you and for my own personal benefit. Telling your story is a great way to remind yourself how far you've come. I also hoped it would motivate readers and explain some important lessons about life and business.

As this book will repeatedly emphasize, the importance of knowing *now* what you knew *then*, and applying those lessons along the way is critical to your success. The basic rules of thumb I learned as a kid still apply, so I'm going to share them with you!

My successful life and career reflect the decisions I made, and these decisions are a result of character. Character develops in your early years in great part through the influence of your family. Consequently, it's important to reflect on lessons learned and how they influence your development. It's easy to see how my outcomes have been a direct result of these Principles at work in my life.

CHAPTER 1

The Impact of Early Influences

Believing that Principle 1—Learn It—starts early in life, it's important to know where I came from.

My parents were the most influential people in my early life. *They were workers with servant hearts who lived their life for others.*

We weren't wealthy, and my parents did what they had to do to get by. Neither ever worked an eight-to-five job. It was more like five-to-eight. They were up at 5:00 a.m. and often not home until after dark, but they were always there when I needed them.

My mom was an incredible cook. It was her passion, her calling. Despite never graduating high school, she was known and respected for using her talent to serve others.

Character is formed early in life from your experiences, beliefs, and the influences around you. Your character defines you.

She always made sure everyone was fed. In addition to all the time she spent raising my brother and me, she worked for a while in the school cafeteria. She was often hired to cook bigger meals like Thanksgiving dinners for other families. She didn't care about the money. She was just doing what she loved.

My dad was a hard worker, dedicated to his employer, and committed to caring for his family. I only remember him having three jobs. Looking back, I can see how each had a major influence on my personal development.

The Gas Man

The first job I remember my dad holding was at a produce distribution center in New Orleans. He was a dedicated and loyal employee for many years, but because of the failing health of my grandparents he decided to move us to Columbia, Mississippi, to be closer to them. It was a difficult decision to leave a company he loved—even as a kid I recognized that—but family was more important (a lesson I would come to appreciate fully in 2003). But looking back, I see other valuable lessons.

We moved to Mississippi, and settled into a house trailer on my grandfather's land. One day, Dad's former boss visited, and I found him in the yard looking at our trailer's hitch. I asked him, "Mr. Sam, what are you doing?"

He replied, "I'm here to see how I can pull this trailer back to New Orleans."

Soon after that visit, Dad starting driving to and from New Orleans for several years—an hour and a half each way, every day—to return to work for Mr. Sam. My dad was loyal to his company, and Mr. Sam repeatedly proved his loyalty to my dad in return.

That's how my dad lived his life. He was loyal to his employers, but more importantly, he was loyal to those he served.

He continued commuting back and forth to New Orleans until he could no longer physically handle the drive and the distance from his family. After that, he took a job as a janitor at a local school. He hated that job, but he did what it took to provide for his family until he found a job that better fit his skills.

His next job, which he held for most of my teenage years, was driving a propane gas truck. He loved this work and soon became known as "The Gas Man." Many days he worked from sunup to sundown, he worked holidays, and sometimes even in the middle of the night. After he delivered the propane, he still had to balance the books, manage the cash, and file the paperwork.

I rode with him many times, and even got to help pump the gas. Often I watched him fill the tanks even when his customers couldn't afford to pay. I'm still not sure how he did it, but he always managed to balance his books while helping those who couldn't afford the gas. He couldn't bear to see them cold or unable to cook, and he said they always paid him later.

I'm sure some of them did, but I'm also sure my dad found a way to pay some of their bills himself. He believed it was the right thing to do, and he simply wanted to help (never mind that he couldn't afford it, either).

My Parent's Legacy

Mom died at the age of seventy-four in 2007; dad died two years later in 2009 at age eighty. Through their last days, they remained proud people. They would not allow me to pay for things they needed but couldn't afford. The only way I could get them to take their medication was to convince them it was paid for by their Medicare supplemental insurance. In reality, it was charged each month to my credit card, which I put on file at their local pharmacy.

I'm happy to say they both got to see me grow from a boy into a young man and adult carrying on the values they instilled in me. Their story is a good one, and consequently, so is mine. Character is built over time, and is the foundation of all you do.

CHAPTER 2

It Began with a Lawn Mower

When I was a kid, playing softball and riding dirt bikes were my favorite pastimes. Softball was free, but owning a dirt bike wasn't, and I quickly began to realize the role money played in life.

I also began to understand why my parents were always working, trying to provide for my older brother and me. Having a job and making money equated to supporting your family and being able to enjoy your hobbies.

When I was about ten years old, my dad took an extra job cutting the grass at our church. I helped him every Saturday, and soon I was pushing the church's lawnmower and dreaming of the day I'd be allowed to ride the "big one." After a few seasons spent helping him, I asked if I could take over the job.

Most kids try to convince their parents that a pet can teach them responsibility, but I wanted to make money to support my hobbies, and I saw this as the best way to do it. It was time for my first business plan, which wasn't exactly a plan, but more an attempt to convince my dad to let me do the work on my own. I explained how it would teach me responsibility while giving him more time at home. I must have said something right, because soon I was riding the big mower and receiving twenty dollars a week from him.

After about six months, having proved that I could handle it, my dad and the church turned the whole job over to me. Soon I was making three hundred dollars per month and loving it!

With my newfound riches, I purchased a motorcycle, which I learned to ride in the fields around my grandparent's home. My friends and I would spend weekday afternoons building jumping ramps and clearing out trails to ride deeper in the woods. Our considerable efforts resulted in a handy network of racing trails and hill climbing trails. Evel Knievel was my hero. I wanted to be like him, so the jumps continued to grow longer and more daring.

This soon became my Sunday afternoon adventure. My friends and I would gather up after church and ride in the woods for hours. My only other interest was watching mid-south wrestling on Saturday afternoon TV at twelve thirty, and no one could convince me it wasn't real. I would schedule my Saturday grass cutting around this hour, which was the only break I took on Saturdays during my busy season. Junkyard Dog and "Hacksaw" Jim Duggan were among my favorite wrestlers.

I saved most of the money I earned with the exception of purchasing a few used motorcycles, a few used cars, and eventually a Commodore 64 computer.

Expansion Opportunity

Shortly after I began cutting the grass at the church, a few church members started asking me to cut their lawns. At first, the church let me borrow their mowers, but as time went by and more people requested my services, I realized I was going to need to purchase my own equipment.

Invest in yourself. It will be the best investment you ever make.

I looked at all the options and discovered Snapper made the best riding lawnmower money could buy. Unfortunately, it cost more than I had and more than I made.

This was my first experience with borrowing money. Dad explained the responsibility of a loan and the importance of making payments on time. When I walked into the Snapper dealership, signing that loan paperwork made me feel like I had some real responsibility. *I had successfully made my first business investment!*

What I didn't know was that my dad had set it all up before I got there and even co-signed for me. Even then, no one freely offered loans to kids with no credit history or collateral!

That lawnmower lesson was my first introduction to return on investment (ROI). *I didn't have to know a big fancy term like "return on investment" to understand what it meant — the concept just made sense.* If I bought a good, fast lawnmower, I could cut more yards and make more money with fewer headaches while spending less money to keep the mower running.

As I continued attracting business, I began purchasing additional equipment so I could work faster and offer more services. I bought brush clearing equipment and lawn sweepers so I could keep my business going in the slower months. I learned to manage the cash and to buy equipment out of "cash flow." *Of course, I had no idea what cash flow meant.* I just knew I didn't want to go into debt, so I only spent what I was making.

I also learned the importance of customer service and what "value added services" meant. Most of my clients were older people, which suited me just fine. I loved people and enjoyed talking, and so did they. I would spend an hour cutting their yards and then take the time to talk with them while carrying out their trash, watering their plants, or doing whatever else they needed me to do.

I never set a price. I simply told them, "Pay me what it's worth and what you can afford," and I was never disappointed. Again and again, I learned just how much the extra step matters. In fact, sometimes my clients' family members offered to have their children cut their grass for free, but my customers wouldn't have it. We built a relationship, and they enjoyed my visits as much as I did. My business grew because I took those extra steps to build relationships, which led to good pay and also to referrals.

Confronting Mistakes

One Sunday morning when I was about sixteen years old, I arrived at church and immediately noticed that the grass in the front was extremely high. To my horror, I realized I had forgotten to cut the church's lawn! I was so consumed with cutting everyone else's yards that I forgot about my main customer, the one who first gave me a chance and believed in me. The customer who was instrumental in helping me grow my business and even let me borrow equipment wasn't given the appropriate attention or made a priority.

I was disappointed in myself and so embarrassed that I wanted to bury my face and cry. My first reaction was to run home and hide, but instead I went to my dad and asked what I should do.

Instead of telling me, he asked me what I thought I should do.

I didn't know. I let the church down, and wasn't sure how to handle it. The only thing I could think of was to face the man who initially agreed to let me handle the church's lawn.

Right after the morning service, I approached Mr. Dale and told him how sorry I was for not cutting the lawn. I told him I didn't have an excuse and that I wouldn't let it happen again.

I will never forget what he told me: "Please don't. I just left a deacons' meeting where the subject was brought up, and I stood up for you and asked them to give you another chance."

I've never forgotten this lesson. If I had failed to confront my mistake head on and take personal accountability, I would have lost the trust I'd worked so hard to gain.

> Remember the feelings that come with major life events. The desire to repeat—or avoid—those feelings is one of the best lessons ever learned.

Growing Pains

Meanwhile, it became glaringly obvious I couldn't keep up by myself. By my junior year, I was moving quickly from yard to yard to get everything done, and though I was gaining more business, my quality of work and the time I could spend on customer service diminished. I even lost a few customers because I wasn't giving them what they valued most: not the cutting of the lawn, but our conversations and the quality of the job along with those other "value adds."

My solution was to build a team to help me deliver high-quality service. Since I was in high school, I went to my friends and convinced some of them to start helping. This way, they could make some extra money, and I would be free to join them for our weekly Sunday afternoon motorcycle rides.

Once I turned fifteen, my dad began letting me drive his truck as long as I paid for the gas. At sixteen, I bought my first car. It was a used, white Monte Carlo with a turbo.

Soon after that, I acquired a red Camaro, along with several off-road dirt motorcycles. To say I was keenly aware of the benefits of hard work would be an understatement.

But to my chagrin, despite my fleet of mowers and lawn equipment, extra help from my friends, and even with new business coming in, I was still losing a few customers. Why? Because "better, faster, and more" wasn't the answer. Some of my friends didn't feel the same commitment I did, which meant I was still struggling to provide the service my customers had come to expect.

When building a team, everyone needs to be on the same page, providing the same level of service, with the same goal. I needed a team of people who did things the way I did them. But the word "I" needed to become the word "we."

I took another shot at a business plan, and this time it included a vision and mission. Granted, I didn't know that's what it was at the time. I just told my friends that we were going to cut yards and do whatever else customers needed and charge them what they could afford or what they offered and be happy about it.

About this time, I also figured out that we could provide better service if each of us did what we liked and were good at, so I tried to focus on each person's strengths. Some of my friends enjoyed edging more than mowing, so that's what they did. If they were doing what they enjoyed, they did a better job. I moved them around a few times to let them experience all the different tasks, but in the end, it was never more than just a job to most of them. They liked the money, but they never felt the same passion for the business that I did.

Teamwork Requires the Right Team

Lesson learned: a *team* consists of a group of people doing a job. A *good team* is a group of people doing what they like for the betterment of the team while doing the job. A *great team* is a group of people respecting other team members and the value they bring to the team while doing the job.

My team was good, but we never became a great team because the work just wasn't as important to my friends as it was to me.

Nonetheless, values, a vision, and mission for what to do and how to do it guided me instinctively. Looking back, it's clear that this period from ages twelve to eighteen established the framework I've used my entire professional life. Those early years were when so many critical relationships started, so many people touched my life, and I developed the character that would guide me in the choices I made afterward.

My experiences developed my beliefs, and my beliefs led to actions, results, and accomplishments, all because I took personal accountability and invested in myself.

CHAPTER 3

It's All About the Tie

Riding around on a lawnmower in southern Mississippi on hot summer days, my mind tended to wander. Not surprisingly, the older I got, the more I began thinking about my future and what might be next. What was I capable of? What could I do better?

The need to maintain and repair my lawnmowers and equipment was improving my mechanical skills, but was this what I wanted to do for the rest of my life? I'd developed a successful business that paid for my hobbies, and I'd even saved up enough to attend the local college, but was this the right place for me?

My older brother never went to college, nor did my parents. At the time, going to college wasn't a given for most kids. No one I knew had college funds or savings plans, and everyone knew college was expensive.

What I did know was that I no longer wanted to spend each day working outside in the sun. By my senior year of high school, I'd decided that an inside, air conditioned job was the job for me, one that allowed me to dress up a bit and maybe wear my Sunday best and a tie. My dad's boss wore a tie, and to me, a tie meant you were a professional and that's what I wanted to be.

Thus was born my first long-term goal: *to wear a tie to work.*

I set a goal without even realizing it. What's more, I set a SMART goal, even though I had no clue what SMART goals were. Actually, they probably weren't even called SMART goals then, but I did it anyway. I did it instinctively.

> It's all about the tie—whatever your tie may be. See your future and set your goals to get there.

Goals Require Objectives

George T. Doran is given credit for introducing SMART Goals in the November 1981 issue of *Management Review*, but the words within the acronym have varied over time.

Specific	Wear a tie to work.
Measurable	Am I wearing a tie to work?
Attainable	Are there jobs out there that involve wearing a tie?
Reasonable/ Relevant	Yes, it is reasonable to find a job that involves wearing a tie.
Time bound	I want to find this job within a month of graduation.

I also needed to set objectives. In fact, the most important part of accomplishing a goal is setting good objectives and identifying the steps needed to achieve the goal.

I knew that in order to meet my goal of wearing a tie to work, I must accomplish a few key tasks along the way:

- Make good enough grades in high school to be accepted into college.
- Earn enough money to pay for college.
- Select a degree that would lead to a job that required wearing a tie.
- Study and do well in college in order to get job interviews.

Only then could I find the job that would accomplish my goal.

Looking back, "wear a tie to work" was a pretty basic goal, but in my mind, a tie represented a professional, well-respected position that paid good money. A tie would mean I was successful, and that made the college decision easier—I would need a college education to get a job that required a tie. So, I was going to college.

The money I'd made mowing yards allowed me to enroll in junior college, but I still needed to decide what degree to go after. Being an average student at best, I felt my options were limited. After meeting with college counselors and assessing my skills, I decided to learn electronics so that I could repair copiers and office equipment. Computers were becoming popular, so I also purchased my Commodore 64 computer and learned basic programming. Buying that computer was one of my best decisions as it led to my love of computers and technology.

I wasn't considered a geek in high school. I played football and loved softball. However, I played football mostly just to be part of a team. But I was intrigued by how that little computer box worked. I enjoyed playing with that computer, and programming fireworks to display on the screen and making balls bounce around was fun.

In 1985, after two years of college, I was out of money and needed to decide what to do next. I lived in the college dorm my first year with the assistance of a government grant, but returned home on the weekends to continue cutting yards for some of my loyal customers. I decided to move home for my second year and commuted two and half hours a day to college. Carpooling with friends helped cut my gas expense.

Earning my associate's degree and finishing first in my electronics class gave me a few options. With personal computers becoming ever more popular, I decided to look into the computer field rather than pursue copier repair.

I turned down two jobs in unrelated fields and continued searching for the job that would meet my goal of wearing a tie to work. One job was 350 miles away in East Texas. It paid more than twice as much as the job I eventually took, but it just wasn't what I wanted. Working in the oil fields outside in the heat did not meet my goal!

The last week of class, my hope of finding a job was dwindling. Fortunately, one of my classmates walked in and said, "I just turned down a job at the hospital in Hattiesburg, Mississippi because they wanted me to wear a dress shirt and tie to work."

My interest piqued. After quizzing my classmate, I called the hospital and asked for an interview.

I was thrilled to accept an entry-level position as a medical electronics technician making five dollars and seventy-five cents per hour. Who knew at age twenty, you could work in a hospital, fix medical equipment, work directly with doctors and nurses, and see live surgeries, all while wearing a tie?

> It not about the money. Don't make it about the money. Make it about the purpose, the results, the why.

What's Your Tie?

What is it that gets you out of bed in the morning?

Is it:
- The corner office,
- A fancy title,
- Serving people,
- Doing charity work,
- Mentoring young people,
- Raising a family?

Maybe it's:

- Starting a new business,
- Losing ten pounds,
- Leaving a job you don't love.

Have you set the SMART goals and objectives to get you there? I'm still amazed that my simple goal of wearing a tie led to an amazing industry where I would spend the next thirty years.

CHAPTER 4

The School of Hard Knocks

Becoming a medical electronics technician turned out to be my dream job. In spite of my young age, I worked on equipment that saved people's lives, I was a respected member of a team, and most importantly, I was wearing a tie to work.

In hindsight, the school of hard knocks was the right school for me. I was always a practical thinker rather than a book smart kind of person. My education came in the form of relentless work, long hours, and learning from other people about what to do and not do. For example, when I watched someone behave in a way that negatively affected other people, I learned to find a better way to handle similar situations.

My family was proud of me, and my dad gave me some great advice the day I told him about my new job. He said, "Son, remember to always be worth more to your employer than the money you receive."

It took me many years to fully understand what he meant, but this statement has helped me keep my

> *Always bring value to your work. Be worth more than the paycheck you receive.*

priorities in order. I've used his advice many times with different twists: I never took a job just for the money, money was never my driving factor, money never made my decisions for me, and I always did my best, believing the money would follow.

I learned a lot from my first official job, and I applied what I'd learned from my dad and in my lawn cutting business to always give extra effort and value adds. Where my new job differed was that in addition to customers, I now had a boss, coworkers, and a company to please. The challenge became how to balance it all while still enjoying the work.

Mastering the Work

My primary goal was to become proficient at my new job. "Learn it" was my first principal of success, and I embraced it wholeheartedly. If I didn't know what I was doing, I wasn't going to make anyone happy. Consequently, I put every effort into learning and then mastering my work while using my skills of talking to people as an added value. I was hired to fix medical equipment, but I took it to the next level. To fix the equipment, I realized it often required me to fix the user as well.

In other words, I was tasked to figure out what users were seeing and doing before I could understand what the problem was. The majority of the time, the issue centered around how the equipment was being used rather than with any fault in the equipment.

I learned how to tell highly trained, highly educated users that they were wrong without ever saying so. I could deliver the message with a smile and an approach that saved their pride. This was truly customer service with a smile. I even grew a mustache to make me appear older than my twenty years so I would be taken more seriously.

Today, making the rounds is standard practice in the medical equipment service industry, but back then, it wasn't the norm. Typically, you sat in the shop, which was almost always in the basement of the hospital, and waited for the phone to ring.

I found this boring, so every morning, I began walking around to each department and asking people if they were having any problems. As my technical skills improved, I realized that I could fix just about any piece of equipment. Likewise, as my communication skills improved, I realized that I could head trouble off by letting people know I understood the issues they were having and assuring them I could address their equipment needs.

I was being proactive, although I didn't know that was the term. These actions not only helped me build relationships, but they also allowed me to fix minor equipment issues before they ballooned into something more serious. Building these relationships before issues arose made for much calmer and easier conversations when problems did arise, with correspondingly high stress levels.

Before long, our department began receiving higher customer satisfaction scores than ever before. My boss was happy and so were my coworkers, who weren't getting as many frantic phone calls from customers.

As for me, once again, I was fully realizing the importance of relationships. This became one of my earliest professional lessons: it's all about relationships.

The Chance to Advance

One day about two years into my job, during my daily rounds, a nurse I often worked with pulled me aside. She asked if I would be willing to meet with her son-in-law about a medical equipment field service job in Texas.

"No way," was my reply. "I love what I'm doing."

Remember Principle 2 — Love It? I did love what I was doing, and besides, this job kept me close to my longtime girlfriend, Brenda, who was now a senior in high school and about to become my fiancé.

This nurse kept after me for several days, trying to convince me to talk to her son-in-law, and finally I agreed to have lunch with him. To be honest, I mainly did it to get a free lunch, since I had no intention of taking the job or moving to Texas.

The lunch meeting was interesting. I learned they were a small company with only four employees, yet they seemed to have big growth plans and were looking for a team of bright young people to train. They had been in business for several years and supported many hospitals in East Texas. The work would be similar to what I was already doing, but would put me at a different location each day rather than being assigned to one hospital. They also were maintaining equipment I wasn't familiar with and would never get to work on in my current job. Even though I was noncommittal, I received an invitation to visit their home office in Longview, Texas, and meet the CEO.

I decided the opportunity was too good to pass up and that the interview would be a good growth experience, so I went.

The CEO spent a lot of time selling me on his company. His excitement and passion about the future of his industry was intense, and I walked away from the interview feeling even more excited about the work I was doing. When he offered me a job, I told him I would think about it, but never intended to accept.

Word Travels Fast

When I returned to work the next day, I was called into my boss's office.

I cringed when he told me he'd heard through the grapevine that I was looking at another job. I was afraid he was going to fire me, but instead, we met with the human resources manager and the CEO of the hospital. Rather than a reprimand, I was offered a raise of fifteen cents per hour to stay.

I thought this was quite a compliment. After all, I'd never intended to leave.

On the way back to the shop, my boss pulled me aside and said something I'll never forget: "Son, you are better than this place. I don't want you to leave, but you have a great future ahead of you. Please don't let other people stand in your way of accomplishing great things."

I was confused. If he wanted me to stay, why was he encouraging me to leave?

That night when I got home, the CEO of the company in Texas called to ask what I thought of the visit. We talked for a while and I'm not sure why I did it, but I accepted the offer on the phone that night. I had no good reason for doing it: I was doing well. I was happy at my job, living at home with my parents, and able to see Brenda every night. We planned to get married in a few months, and I had purchased a brand-new car and was saving a little money for a house. I put in my two-week notice and moved from Columbia, Mississippi to Longview, Texas in 1986.

Open minds lead to open roads. You'll never know where you might go unless you're willing to accept the opportunity to change.

A few months later, during a trip back home to Mississippi, I dropped in to see my old boss. I asked him why he encouraged me to leave. He told me he saw something in me I didn't even see in myself—potential. He explained that he wanted me to stay but felt a field service job better fit my personality and gave me more career opportunities.

When I look back now, I'm amazed and humbled that he put my future ahead of his own needs.

What Comes Around, Goes Around

On another trip home months later, I ran into the nurse who referred me to the job in Longview. I asked her why she encouraged me to pursue the new opportunity and she said the same thing. She saw potential in me and believed the job change would help me grow. These are the kind of people you remember in your lifetime — the ones that touched you and didn't even know it.

Writing this book brought her back to mind, and I reached out to her. After thirty years, she still remembered me, though the details of our last conversation are clearer to me than to her. As we talked and I told her what a difference her belief in me made in my early career, it became clear she had no idea how she touched my life. I could hear the surprise and emotion in her voice as we talked about it. We both hung up the phone feeling happy — her for learning she made a difference and me for being able to share it.

I never would have imagined the nurse I talked to every day as I walked around the hospital would be instrumental in a major career change, or that my boss would encourage me to take another job that would benefit me so much.

I also never envisioned that years later I would return to visit the same CEO who had offered me a small pay increase to stay on at that first job. Making a presentation for that hospital representing my own company was a highlight of my career. He remembered me and told me how proud he was of me.

My upbringing had taught me to treat everyone I met with respect, and once again, it was paying off.

Subsequently, I made a point of telling people who worked for me that if they ever felt there was a better opportunity out there, to please go after it. I never wanted to stand in the way of anyone's dreams or potential to take care of his or her families.

If you want to be respected, start by showing respect to others.

Once I started my own business, there were many occasions when people did leave the company for various reasons. Over the years, some of them either returned to my company or referred other customers or employees to me. When people know you are sincerely looking out for them, you earn a higher level of respect.

This rule of thumb still applies. You just never know when the person you're talking to at any given moment may cross your path again, or help you somewhere down the road.

CHAPTER 5

Moving Out of My Comfort Zone

Moving more than 350 miles away from my family, my childhood sweetheart, and all my friends was going to be tough. I'd only been to East Texas once — during my interview with the CEO in Longview. In fact, I'd only been in three states by age eighteen: Mississippi, Louisiana, and Alabama. I was literally moving out of my comfort zone, something no one in my immediate family had done before.

My mom and dad told me it was my decision, but I knew in their hearts they didn't want me to go. My brother is eight years older, and we were not close. By this time, he was already married and out of the house, so my decision would leave them with an empty nest.

Brenda fully supported this decision, even though we were about nine months away from our wedding day and had planned to live in a house trailer on a few acres of land on a hill above my parent's house in Columbia, Mississippi.

This wasn't much of a plan, but it was as far as we'd gotten. I think we figured that as long as we had love, we had all we needed. My new job would change all our plans, but Brenda was game.

My Best Girl

I remember the day we met in 1982 — or at least the day I saw Brenda in the school cafeteria during lunch. I asked my friend who she was, and he told me her name was Brenda and that she went to his church. He invited me to go to church with him the next Sunday and said he'd introduce me.

I was hooked from that moment, even though she was four years younger than I was, something I didn't know at the time; I was seventeen and she was just thirteen.

She was too young to date, but her mom allowed me to come over to her house for spaghetti, and thus began a year of many "house dates." We would spend our time at each other's house eating dinner, watching TV, and playing Atari video games. Our favorite date night was playing the Mattel handheld football game, which was no more than dots on a small screen. Brenda prided herself on beating me all the time.

Her mom later told me that the only reason she allowed me to come over was that she'd heard I was a good kid. Thank heavens for all the relationships I'd built, and for my good reputation!

By the time I moved to Longview, Brenda and I had been dating almost four years and had been engaged for two. Deep down, though neither of us would admit it, we both felt the time apart would do us good. Neither of us had ever seriously dated anyone else, and it seemed like a good idea to spend some time on our own before we married.

I started my new job as a field service technician in that small company as employee number five. I figured it was a great opportunity to learn and grow and be in on the ground floor. The people who worked there seemed happy and like a big family. The company had a plan to grow beyond East Texas. I was assigned to cover several small hospitals and I thought if I could learn quickly and get as much experience as possible, I would be able to advance quickly.

During my move, I couldn't help but smile, recalling the job in the oil fields I'd been offered right out of college. It was in the same town I was moving to now. It still paid twice the money I was about to make, but I didn't care. I wasn't going to have to work outside in the hot sun, and I *was* going to get to wear a tie.

Follow your passion.

It wasn't about the corner office or a fancy title. I didn't consider myself ambitious, but I did want more out of life. Advancing in my career would allow me to accomplish this.

Moving to Texas turned out to be a good decision, but it also introduced me to my first significant personal and professional challenges, including:

- Being so far away from Brenda and my family,
- Working horribly long hours,

- Driving many miles to see customers,
- Learning to care for equipment I wasn't familiar with.

Since I had no distractions, I spent all my time on work. I quickly became well versed in all aspects of my profession. I discovered there are no limitations to what can be accomplished with hard work and a team of like-minded people.

I worked many hours with no overtime pay (overtime compensation didn't exist at that time in that particular field), and I made myself worth much more than I ever received in compensation. I made a point of being one of the last employees to get home each night, believing that if I focused on the job and my own performance, the compensation would come.

I was following my dad's advice from years earlier, and, I was wearing a tie! When asked to work on equipment that I had no idea how to use, my favorite statement became "Show me what it's not doing." This allowed me to observe the operator while learning what the equipment was supposed to do, so I could start troubleshooting. Time and again, I was put into situations with angry operators and department managers only to walk out with them smiling and thanking me for fixing their equipment.

Once again, my technical skills were on the rise. I truly enjoyed the challenges, and continued to pay close attention to the people I worked for (and with) to learn and grow as much as possible.

I liked living in Texas and meeting new friends, although most were coworkers since I worked about twelve hours a day. I loved my job and the company. I assumed this would be where I retired, and never dreamed of working anywhere else. I had all I ever wanted: a great job, I was wearing a tie, and working for a company I believed in. My salary had increased fairly quickly and my experience was expanding beyond any expectations. I was being given a lot of responsibility and learning way more than I expected. I was building relationships by treating people with respect and doing the right thing. I had become a trusted employee of the owner and felt ownership in the company. It's like I had become part of his family. Little did I know, my happy, comfortable world was about to be challenged. Sometimes I think life throws you curves to see how you will handle them.

Ticking Time Bomb

Leaving my family and fiancé back in Mississippi allowed me to progress in my career, but my schedule was taxing. I drove about a thousand miles a week making service calls and then another seven hundred miles every other weekend to visit Brenda and my family. Because I worked for a company that cared about me and because I'd built personal relationships with my customers, I was allowed to head out a little early every other Friday. After all, everyone knew I was heading home to see Brenda (and my family, of course).

I love telling stories to make a point. The stories are almost always true, but as with good fishing stories, they seem to grow over time.

Remember I said you never know when the little decisions you make and the relationships you build will change your life?

One day, a service call came from one of my hospitals in Louisiana, and my boss sent me out early on a Friday morning to address the problem on my way home to Mississippi. This was a Lifepak 6 defibrillator (an EKG monitor), a piece of equipment I could fix with my eyes closed. It should be a routine quick fix that should take less than thirty minutes.

> Everything is about relationships. Put in the time and effort to build them, and then don't burn them.

When I arrived at the hospital, I met my normal contact, and he told me the equipment was in the outpatient center. I proceeded to the repair, but after almost two hours, the job wasn't done.

When my contact asked how things were going, he clearly saw the frustration on my face. He knew I was heading home to see my sweetheart. Because of the relationship we'd built, he told me to take the equipment with me, fix it at home, and deliver it on Sunday night on my way back through town. His seemingly insignificant decision to allow me to take that monitor for the weekend made an amazing difference in my life.

Even though I'd moved to Texas almost a year earlier, I still cut grass for a few loyal customers on weekends when I was home, and Brenda always helped me.

Saturday morning, after we finished the yards, I went back to the monitor repair and fixed the problem in less than five minutes. Turns out the problem was a battery lead, something I should have found quickly the day before, but that's not the amazing part.

Brenda was curious to know what this contraption did. Wanting to impress her, I connected her to the monitor so she could see her heartbeat.

By now, I'd learned how the equipment was used in addition to learning how to repair it, and here's where the amazing part comes in.

Looking at the EKG, I was stunned to see that Brenda had a significant heart block.

She was now a senior in high school and an incredible basketball player fully expecting to receive a basketball scholarship to play in college. She was All-Conference and All-State, but felt tired all the time. During a practice that year, she'd passed out on the court.

Everyone thought she was depressed because her fiancé had moved 350 miles away to Texas. No one considered that she might have a medical problem, much less a serious heart condition. She was a strong athlete and a seemingly healthy teenager.

I printed the EKG strip showing the second-degree heart blockage, gave it to Brenda's mother, and left on Sunday to deliver the equipment to the hospital in Louisiana and return to Texas.

By Wednesday, I was back in Mississippi for Brenda's surgery. She needed a permanent pacemaker. The doctors told us later that if we hadn't caught the heart problem, she probably would have died in her sleep due to a severe second-degree heart blockage.

Thanks to the relationships I had with hospital personnel in Mississippi, I was permitted to watch part of the procedure to install Brenda's pacemaker.

Having an experience like this at the age of twenty-one is eye opening. It gives you an appreciation of life and reminds you just how short it can be.

When I tell this story, I always end it this way: Brenda married me because I saved her life. That might be a bit of stretch, but it's how I like to think of it.

Until Death Do Us Part

On June 6, 1987, Brenda became my wife and moved to East Texas with me.

This was hard on her parents. It was only a few months after her pacemaker procedure, but we were determined and committed. Besides, I was the one who had discovered her heart condition. I was certain I could take care of her.

The CEO of the company I worked for surprised us when he and his wife showed up at our wedding. We had planned a short honeymoon to Branson, Missouri, while pulling a trailer behind us with all of our belongings. My boss gave me the keys to his much nicer car and told us he had paid for a reservation at a nice hotel in Jackson, Mississippi, where we were to have dinner on him.

After a brief visit with our family and friends we departed on our new journey. I was looking forward to not having to drive back every other weekend to Mississippi to visit her. Little did I know at the time that the long drive would continue for another year because she missed home and often wanted to go back to visit. The trips were much easier though with my new bride riding alongside me.

> Loyalty is vital to strong relationships. It is built over time from little things that have great value.

Brenda and I had never stayed at a nice hotel before, and we didn't eat fancy meals, so we didn't know what to do. We ordered room service — cheeseburgers with fries — and decided to celebrate with a glass of champagne.

We weren't drinkers and didn't know one bottle of champagne from another, so I ordered the cheapest on the menu. Room service called back shortly and said they were out of that one and would I like another type. I asked for the only name I recognized: Dom Perignon.

Imagine our surprise when we received the bill for two twenty-dollar cheeseburgers with a two hundred-dollar bottle of champagne!

Young and innocent, we continued on our honeymoon trip, worried sick about how we were going to pay my boss back.

When I called to check in at the office, I heard it had been a hard week, so we decided to return to Texas a day early.

Looking back, our move to Texas couldn't have been easy on Brenda. We got home on Thursday night, spent our first night together in our new place, and I got up early Friday morning and went to work, leaving her all alone in a strange town. Although I loved Brenda with all my heart, I hadn't learned the concept of "family first" yet.

When I gave my boss the receipt for our expensive meal, I told him I'd pay him back if he'd hold the money out of my next year's pay. He laughed and told me not to worry and asked if we'd enjoyed the champagne.

I couldn't help but tell him the truth—it wasn't that great, but we'd really appreciated it. Brenda and I didn't drink alcohol growing up, so it only took one glass for us to feel the effects.

Meanwhile, I discovered my team was stressed. I was the area supervisor and still working in the hospitals. The supervisor role was not a formal role; we were a small company and titles didn't matter. All it meant was I was responsible for organizing schedules. They'd covered for me all week, and since it had been a heck of a week, I volunteered to be on call to give them a break over the weekend. I like telling this story because it indoctrinated Brenda right off the bat into the kind of work I did and what was to come.

Friday night, as soon as we'd gone to sleep, my pager went off. It was a call at a small hospital two hours away. The thought of staying by herself at night on only her second night in a new place terrified Brenda. Thanks to the relationships I'd built, most of my customers already knew about Brenda, so I decided it was okay if she tagged along with me.

That evening, she began to see firsthand what I did for a living. We walked into a small hospital, and a stressful situation with a critical piece of equipment down. Brenda sat in the corner, watching. When the lab tech came out to greet me, she turned out to be a very cute girl who came right up and gave me a big hug just for showing up.

On the way home, Brenda asked if it was always like this.

I told her this job was 24-7 and that if you did good work, you were appreciated, but I think she was talking about the girl.

In the end, this experience helped Brenda understand and buy into the culture of the company. On days I felt stressed, she would pick me up by reminding me what a good company "we" worked for. We became involved in company get-togethers and hosted many in our home. When I was involved in employee interviews, she wanted to be part of the process. She felt as much a part of the company as I did.

The only time she didn't automatically support me occurred five years later, when the moving truck pulled up to move us to Dallas. Our fast-growing company had now reached about thirty employees, and the home office was moving to Dallas to establish a more viable national presence. The company was attempting to define a more corporate structure preparing for growth. I was being promoted to a full-time sales role in business development, so we were moving, too.

She sat on the porch of our Longview home and said, "I'm not going."

Although we weren't leaving a lot behind in Longview, the move was tough on her. Our first son, Brice, was about a year old. We didn't have any friends outside of work and most of them would be moving as well. The house we had purchased on our first anniversary sold within a couple months. She loved her job at the car dealership, and thanks to their recommendation she was already committed to a similar job at a new dealership in Dallas. It was just change. While I embraced change, Brenda hated change. Nonetheless, at the end of the day, she always supported me, and this time was no exception. She trusted and believed in me.

By the time that truck was loaded and ready to pull out, she was sitting by my side.

Navigating Change

Change. It's a simple, but powerful word. Change is a huge part of accomplishing success. Change, although not always good, is necessary to move forward not only in professional life, but your personal life as well.

When you're asked to change, try to understand the "why" behind the change. Approach the change with an open attitude—it can make all the difference.

Accepting and embracing change can be challenging for some people. They question the need for change. Creating change and helping others accept it is a vital quality to being a great leader. Answering the "why" for a change can be the best way to help change-averse people accept it.

I have a few pieces of advice to offer to help facilitate change:

- If you're the one driving the change (or you've accepted the change), understand that others are likely to be reluctant to change. If change is being forced on you, try approaching it with an open mind and seeing it from another point of view.

- If you're driving change, focus on the bigger goal—the "why" for the change. If you're being asked to change, focus on one small step at a time. Sometimes change is easier to accept in smaller bites.

- If you're driving change, be sure to share the long-term benefits of the change—how it will help your team, make life better, etc. If you're being asked to change, accept your personal role in the change process.

- If you're driving change, sometimes you have to be willing to take a couple of steps backward in order to move forward. Change may not happen easily. If you're being asked to make a change, look for the positives rather than focusing on what is going or could go wrong.

Trust is an important component of the willingness to change. Take time to build trust with your team, family, or partner before it's time to change. When someone asks you to change, be willing.

CHAPTER 6

Leading by Example

When I finally became a manager, I received one of the biggest, most shocking lessons of my life. It knocked me back on my heels and to this day I'm almost embarrassed to admit how wrong I was. Since then, I've discovered a lot of rising young stars make the same mistake, so read on with care.

In 1989, at age twenty-four, I was responsible for a large territory with several people reporting to me. I was learning to become a better leader. Each day, I embodied Principle 3—Live It. Working in a small company, even as a manager you still have to do the work. I was a manager, but with a hands-on style of working alongside my team. I enjoyed this part of the job because I got to lead by example to prove to new employees I had been there and done it. This helped build my credibility. I was still fixing equipment when needed and keeping my technical expertise updated. Not only did I help develop a training program for new hires and people who wanted

Learn to serve before you try to lead. Leaders serve first.

to change industries, but I also began to hire new technicians for our growing company, and played a vital role in acquiring new business.

I knew that I had to continue to be technically competent if I wanted to grow in my career, so I took the hardest jobs and was always the last one home at night. Even as I continued to advance, it was still a small company and I wanted to stay involved in the day-to-day operations. This allowed me to see the most difficult repairs and the customers who were most upset. In the medical equipment world, equipment must be ready to use at all times. If the equipment fails, personnel can't do their jobs and patient care suffers.

I became more technically proficient and developed better teamwork skills. In turn, this improved my leadership skills. Taking these extra steps earned the respect of my teammates. When I needed them, they were always supportive. It made a big difference as I was promoted to supervisor of more and more peers.

Having their respect first was essential. When they had to report to me, our relationship was formed and they knew I cared about their best interests. I was excited about my new promotion to manager, and the subsequent move to Dallas with the company. I felt I was ready to take this step, but little did I know that it would turn out to be a bigger challenge than I'd expected.

Bigger Than My Britches

I thought that when I became a manager, people would just do what I told them to do because I was their boss, but man, did I approach this wrong. Instead of continuing to do things the way I'd always done them, which was why my boss had given me the job, I let my promotion go to my head. The unfortunate result was that I lost the respect of some of my peers that I'd worked so hard to gain. As a young and inexperienced manager, I became bossy and got a little too big for my britches. I acted like I was better than everyone else — after all, I was the boss. I quickly learned this approach wasn't going to work. Instead, I learned to manage to my strength, which was leadership. Working well with people and building solid relationships are fundamental qualities of a good leader.

Management, simply put, requires an understanding of how to deal with processes. When I first entered management, I focused on processes, like time sheets and assignments, and making sure quality service was being performed. That style wasn't going to allow me to be a good manager without first being a great leader. Leading and guiding and working with people was what had gotten me to where I was in my career, so when I tried to manage without offering any leadership it just didn't work.

I learned the hard way that you *manage* things and *lead* people, that you work *with* people, not *through* them, and that you *ask*, not *tell*. I also learned that you lead by example and don't ask someone to do something you would never do yourself. My "school of hard knocks" lessons continued through my first years of learning to manage and lead people.

It's hard not to think about money when you're young and struggling to pay your bills, but I did a pretty good job of focusing on my work rather than my coworkers' pay until I moved into management. Once I began supervising ten people, I naturally thought I should be making more money than they did. Once again, I found out how wrong I was.

My boss hired a technician who reported to me. When I found out he was making more than I was, I was upset because I was working so many hours not only supporting my customers but also helping everyone else with their customers. Now a new guy comes along and gets paid more than me? My emotions showed and finally, my boss sat me down and asked, "Do you want to be a great leader or just a worker the rest of your career?"

The answer was easy. Of course I wanted to continue to grow and be a good manager and eventually a great leader.

His reply was simple. "Well then, grow up and realize that in order to be successful in the long term, you need a competent team around you."

I got it. Sometimes I had to hire and manage people who had more experience and made more money than I did.

This reinforced what my dad had always told me: be worth more than you're being paid. Once I accepted this simple philosophy, I began to focus on making good decisions rather than on bottom-line financials. I became more concerned with doing the right thing instead of doing the cheapest thing.

Going Corporate

Once the home office was established in Dallas in 1992, we faced the challenge of keeping all employees on the same page. Growth is good, but it needs to be managed. Often, people lose sight of what got them where they are, which hinders their growth and decision-making abilities. In our company, it quickly became apparent that keeping everyone focused on the same objective would be a problem. The company had grown to the point that we had accounts and employees in several states.

It seemed we had developed an "us versus them" attitude. It was "management" and the "field personnel." We were no longer one team. It felt like management expected the field personnel to be there to support them, rather than management existing to support the field, as it should be. Communication to the field personnel was being limited and protected. Overall, the company had forgotten who was most important. The working environment became more secretive and closed-door, very unlike the way it used to be.

Meanwhile, I faced a major watershed moment in my career. I realized these changes meant that I might have lost what had made me so good at my job and what had made me successful.

It's important to remember what got you where you are. Always stay humble.

My strengths as a leader included treating everyone with respect and giving others a feeling of ownership which helped them do a better job and work together toward a shared goal. Passion for my job and the industry had always driven me, but in 1994, I realized I had lost that passion and direction. It was beginning to affect my professional and personal life.

A few years earlier, the company leadership had recognized the challenges that come with a growing business. There was a need to balance the operational knowledge of the current leadership with someone who had a strong business background. Unfortunately, that resulted in a director of operations who ran things with a more controlling, heavy-handed approach than I was used to.

I had a great relationship with the employees and was being called every day with complaints about how they were being treated. But I was a company man so I continued to defend the corporate actions. It was tough not to tell the employees how I felt.

I've always worn my feelings on my sleeve, so I'm sure everyone could see right through my mask. I supported where we were going as a company and was doing my best to explain things and keep everyone happy. But it was getting harder for me to continue supporting what I no longer believed in.

My family was being affected by my busy travel schedule and extended absences. Although I was considered business development, the majority of my time was spent on operational calls that spanned the entire United States.

Our oldest son Brice was now four, and I felt the need to be home more. I requested to step away from the corporate office and into an operational role running the service program at a large hospital with multiple people reporting to me.

This turned out to be a good decision. It was time to get back to why I did what I did. I'd been the one to bring on this hospital, built a relationship with the administration, and knew what the role would require. It was the largest hospital we had taken on as a company, and I was concerned the client's needs would not be well supported. After all, it was my name on the deal. I felt personally responsible for the agreement.

I regained my focus on why I was in one of the best industries around and why it was important to do good work. Working directly for the people we served and relearning what they wanted from their service partner rejuvenated me and helped me regain enthusiasm for my profession.

A Brief Return to Operations

The hospital embraced me as part of their family even though I was a contracted employee. They treated me like one of their directors (which was a big deal for a contractor) and invited me to department parties. I felt truly accepted as part of their team, and it was great to see and feel their appreciation in return for good service.

Working in a large hospital gave me a new perspective. The hospital management and administration helped me understand how a medical equipment service program should be managed and helped me understand who my customers were through their eyes. It was revealing and changed the way I looked at the business. I had never worked directly in the management of a hospital where I was so heavily involved in the politics of hospital administration. Involving me in their operational structure and treating me as part of their family allowed me to better understand their perspective. They trusted me, and in return they received a higher level of commitment and loyalty from me.

I also gained a much clearer understanding that it sometimes takes additional outside support to truly provide excellent service. Realizing that you can't do everything isn't a weakness; it's actually a strength. In the service world, from a corporate perspective, using outside or subcontracted vendors is often viewed as an expensive option to be avoided. Indeed, service providers sometimes believe they should be superman and handle everything themselves.

Don't be afraid to take a step back in order to go further.

I learned the opposite was true. Spending more money isn't always the way to go. Being smarter about how you work with vendors and focusing on the end result, which is customer satisfaction, means a far bigger payoff for everyone. Getting people on the same page by listening first and then explaining your perspective is the way to achieve a win-win for everyone.

About a year later, a different company took over the contracts due to a corporate-ownership decision, so I moved back into our corporate office in Dallas and resumed my role in business development and sales.

CHAPTER 7

Beginning to Stretch

After moving back to the corporate office, I seemed to be far less involved in company operations. It felt like I was being pushed aside. More meetings were occurring behind closed doors. I lost the feeling of ownership I once felt so fervently.

So in 1994, my quest to rekindle my passion led me to start a side business.

At that time, home computers were still expensive, and so many options were available that the buying process was overwhelming. Most people knew they wanted a computer, but they had no idea what to buy or what to do once they unpacked the box if they did make a purchase. My passion and enthusiasm for personal computers continued to grow and I wanted to do more. Thirsty for knowledge, I loved technology and working with people. Seeing their excitement when something "clicked" was always satisfying.

I opened my new side business, Advantage Computers, to provide custom-built personal home computer systems as well as personalized training and support. I was flying solo and that's what I needed.

Business was good, and I built about twenty computer systems within my first six months, working nights and weekends. I didn't sleep much, but my mind never shuts down anyway.

Paycheck to Paycheck

It was a good hobby, and, as long as I didn't count my time, it even generated a little extra money. However, it was beginning to take more and more of my time, and I was already traveling a lot in my "real job."

I saw a chance to grow the business when a company wanted to lease thirty computers from me. The challenge was that I had to purchase, build, and install them in Pittsburgh, Pennsylvania. To accommodate my regular work schedule, it would have to take place over a three-day, Fourth of July holiday weekend.

This meant purchasing all the parts, traveling to the site, building the computers, setting up and testing them, installing software, and ensuring that the computers were ready to use Monday morning. The associated expenses, including the travel, were to be reimbursed over a six-month lease agreement.

Like almost everyone we knew, Brenda and I were living paycheck to paycheck with little disposable cash, which meant I didn't have the money to do the job. Even though my salary had climbed through the years, it had not kept up with the cost of living, much less supporting a new business.

The bank all but laughed at me and made it clear I'd have to find another way to finance the deal. Finally, I secured a short-term, high-interest loan that I hadn't planned on when I'd submitted my proposal to complete the job. In the end, the job that promised to be a high-profit venture barely broke even.

It was fun building the computers and teaching people who truly had no clue what a computer did. I enjoyed working with people, but seriously underestimated the time commitment to teach a total novice how to work on a computer. Principle 2 was in full gear: I loved the work. But prices began dropping dramatically as computers became more readily available. Besides, the business model of in-home computer support was slightly ahead of its time.

I closed down the company and wrote it off as lessons learned. The main thing I gained was getting my enthusiasm back and renewing my passion. This was my first venture into owning my own business since cutting lawns as a kid. Even though Advantage Computers was short-lived, I learned a lot about business:

Hold yourself accountable; you are responsible for you.

- How to legally set up a company, file taxes, run reports — the paperwork side.

- The challenges of bank financing and securing capital, even for a small amount of money.

- To take the risk — opportunities and the right timing don't come around often; be ready to pursue them when they do.

Most importantly, I was reminded about the value of relationships. Speaking of relationships, let's get back to my most important one.

Back to Brenda

After her heart surgery, Brenda didn't pursue basketball any further. With her heart issues, a scholarship would have been tough to obtain. But she did want to go to college.

After we married and moved to East Texas in 1987 Brenda started classes at Kilgore College. Initially she wanted to be a nurse like her mom. Unfortunately, Brenda is deathly afraid of needles, so she decided to go into accounting instead. She worked her way through school and earned her associate's degree in accounting. She landed a position as an intern at a local car dealership in the accounting department, and worked her way into a full-time position after graduation. She became such a valuable employee at the dealership that when it came time for us to relocate, her boss recommended her to another dealership in the Dallas area.

On a house-hunting trip prior to our official move, we decided to stop by the Dallas dealership just to drop off her resume. Thirty minutes later, Brenda walked out with a job offer. Over the next twelve years, she worked her way up from the accounting department to become the owner's right hand and most trusted assistant.

Although Brenda and I had different personalities, we were raised similarly and shared the same values. Our families only lived about ten miles apart, and her parents also worked hard to make ends meet.

Her mother, Nana — that's what we've called her since our boys were born — was a nurse and worked in the hospital in Columbia, Mississippi until she was offered a job in a private practice. Papa J., so named when the grandkids came along, worked many jobs. The last several years prior to his retirement, he worked in maintenance at the Columbia hospital.

Neither of our parents had much in the way of material possessions, but they always provided for us. Our similar upbringing in the Deep South taught us to appreciate what we had and guided us in how we treated others. These values and her character allowed Brenda to progress quickly in her career.

Brenda always worked. She had worked part-time jobs back in Mississippi and she continued working through college as an intern. She became a full-time employee with that same company after college graduation.

After about three years of marriage, we decided we were ready to start a family. We assumed, like most people do, this would be easy and come naturally. A year and a lot of fertility medications later, Brice was born. As you can imagine, the stress took a toll on every facet of our lives, but the birth of our beautiful boy made it all worthwhile.

Brenda continued working throughout her pregnancy and after Brice was born. Our plan was to have a second child fairly soon thereafter, but again we struggled. It took six years of trying, numerous medications, and several fertility treatments before Braden came along.

Even after Braden was born, Brenda continued working, wanting to make sure we provided well for our family. She has never been the stay-at-home-mom kind of person. Because she has a servant heart, she was always happy working for someone else as long as she felt like she mattered and her work was appreciated. This is a meaningful trait that we both have in common.

Decisions, Decisions

Decisions. Life is full of them, and each one can change your life forever. Making the right decision depends on using all the information you have available to you while keeping your core values in mind, remembering what you know, and how you learned it.

There are easy decisions, such as where to go to lunch, what movie to see, and what to wear. They don't have much impact one way or another, which might be why the common response to them is "I don't care."

Whether or not we realize it, we also make psychological decisions from the moment we open our eyes in the morning to the moment we go to sleep. These include choosing whether or not to have a good day, whether or not to persist in the face of disappointment, whether to value people more than money, and so on.

Then there are the big, material decisions, the ones that change your life. This is when you rely on character, remembering what you learned in the past, and using it make conscious decisions using your moral compass to weigh the options and possible outcomes.

In 1998, after twelve years with that company, I was faced with one of the most difficult decisions I've ever made. The company had changed in a way I couldn't relate to, and I no longer agreed with its philosophy. It seemed to have lost sight of what was important and what had led to its success: people.

I understood this approach could be successful — and sometimes even necessary — in a growing company. However, I didn't like it then and still don't like this management method. I believe we can appreciate each other's strengths. Complementary styles can lead to far more successful relationships. Since I was working out of the corporate office, I quickly grew frustrated with the authoritarian management style. More importantly, I felt like I was no longer following my dad's advice of being worth more than I was paid. Indeed, what was once my career became "just a job." I felt guilty about this.

My passion makes me who I am and that passion was gone. I no longer:

- Enjoyed the drive to work,
- Looked forward to the workday,
- Felt part of the home team, or,
- Felt like my work was appreciated or made a difference.

Plus, the company forgot about the little things that made the business great. Things like spending twenty dollars on something small that leads to exponential

----
Character drives
your decision-
making process.
----

effort and commitment in return. The importance of people feeling their work is appreciated and valued. All the characteristics that made the company great seemed to be lost.

Turning Point

The final straw came when I was out of town on business. Brenda called to let me know Braden was sick. She was scared and wanted me to come home. I was traveling with my boss in the company's private plane. We landed long enough to drop me off and he proceeded to a different city where he wasn't scheduled to return for another two days. When I explained what was going on with Braden, he said he couldn't change his schedule to come get me and wouldn't approve a commercial flight home either. I would have to wait until the next day to return home as scheduled.

I felt hurt and disappointed. This went against everything I felt the company stood for, or at least should stand for.

When I got home and saw Brenda and my son, I made the difficult decision to resign my position. Leaving a company that had taught me so much was by far one of the hardest, most emotionally draining decisions I've ever made. Oddly enough, Brenda and I didn't discuss it much. We had separate careers and didn't talk much about what was going on in our work lives. But she felt the change in me and in the company. She knew I was unhappy with the company's direction. My unhappiness was personally affecting both of us.

I showed her my resignation letter on Sunday night. Monday morning, I drove my company car to the office, sat through a meeting, and then turned in my resignation. I don't think Brenda actually thought I would do it, and I wasn't sure either.

Initially, my boss refused to accept the letter. I think what I was doing shocked both of us. I knew his direction, and for the most part why he was going that way, but I felt I was no longer part of his plan. I know he would not admit it, but I was no longer bringing the value I felt I needed to and a change was the only way to fix it.

My passion was gone, and it seemed that several other people in the company were experiencing the same problem. The relationship of the front-line employees and management had changed within the company and it no longer fit my style.

After we talked at length, he realized I wasn't going to change my mind. I offered him two weeks' notice, but we both knew my decision was made, and he allowed me to leave that day.

I called Brenda to come pick me up. After an emotional farewell to our extended family of twelve years, we drove home. The silence in the car was palpable. The chill outside on that February 1998 day was a pretty good reflection of the chill in our hearts over what had just happened. Twelve years. Now what? We didn't exactly have a plan, but we assumed it would all work out.

That decision was one of the most difficult I ever made. We were leaving a family I had literally grown up with. The company owner was a mentor and a friend. Our kids had played together, and we even lived with his family for a period of time during the transition to Dallas. However, at the end of the day, I had to make the decision that was right for my family and me.

CHAPTER 8

Climbing the Ladder

I learned many things in my twelve years with that company and had progressed from technician to running operations and then into sales. I played a valuable role in a growing company where I was able to learn many things, the most important being how to treat people. Roles or titles never mattered to me. I always did whatever was needed of me.

My true passion was building customer relationships and working with the employees. Running training programs, introducing new people to our industry, and teaching them what I knew became my love. I measured success by each time one of them was hired or promoted and grew in our field. One of my greatest pleasures today continues to be when I hear that someone I trained has done well with their career.

I was working through the five levels of leadership detailed in Jim Collins' book *Good to Great* before I even knew who he was, or had even heard of the book.

Specifically:

- I started my career trying to be the best technician I could be (Level 1).
- I became part of a team of technicians working together (Level 2).
- I became a manager accepting all the challenges that came with it (Level 3).
- I became an effective leader by building a successful team working with people (Level 4).
- I turned my interest into helping others succeed (Level 5).

I learned the hard way, on my own, what all the leadership and management books tell you about how to be a manager and leader. I learned to be what I refer to as a "practical leader" using what I thought was common sense rather than by reading it in a book.

The fact is, I never enjoyed reading, and it didn't come easily for me. Later in life, I learned that I'm severely dyslexic, which explained why reading was always such a challenge. My youngest son, Braden was diagnosed with dyslexia in elementary school and through dealing with his 504 education plans, I discovered that I was also dyslexic.

Dyslexia is a disease of the optic nerve that makes the letters in words look switched around. So "god" may appear like "dog" and my name, "Brian," might look like "Brain." Boys are far more likely to have it than girls. Many people with dyslexia learn to compensate with great people skills and other talents and abilities.

This explained a lot, such as my struggles in school, why it was so hard to write, and why reading was never easy for me. After understanding how dyslexia worked, I became more conscious of my writing. I diligently checked every detail, and the F7 key on the computer became my best friend (that used to be the hot key for spell-check—I'm dating myself).

Lacking a formal business education, I went the route of watching and learning from those around me. I saw what worked and what didn't, and I took a practical, common-sense approach to leadership and management. I learned to get people to perform at their highest level by treating them with respect and making them feel part of something bigger than themselves, and I also tried to understand where they were coming from before I offered my solution.

> Do the right thing, even when it hurts. Every time.

I learned the importance of having empathy for others. I always tried to look at every situation from the other person's point of view. I didn't always agree with them, but it helped me understand where they were coming from or to anticipate how they may respond. When I prepared proposals for new clients, I would first present to myself as the customer and question myself on what I was presenting. This worked with employee issues as well.

Understanding their feelings first always led me to a much better, longer-lasting relationship.

I came to understand that everyone is different and how important this is when building a team. If you know what needs to be done, you can gather all different personalities and strengths to build that team. When that team realizes and appreciates the other members of the team, success can't help but happen.

I learned why you should surround yourself with people who compensate for your own weaknesses. The best advice I can offer is to never be the smartest person in the room.

I tried to show integrity by always doing the right thing, and I talked "Do the right thing" over and over. Sometimes people ask me what this means. How do you know when something is the "right thing"?

Be a person of integrity.

My answer is always the same. It must feel right, which means trust your gut instincts. Others don't always see your idea of "the right thing" the same way. Some of the toughest situations leaders and managers face involve making decisions they feel are "the right thing." This is especially true when making a decision that wasn't "the easy thing" and could have negative implications.

To sum it up, my best advice on doing the right thing is that if it feels right, it probably is. If it feels wrong, it probably is.

Later in life, my ongoing desire to improve myself and develop my skills led me to collect and read numerous leadership and management books. I've included some of my favorites in the resource section of this book.

These books confirmed most of what I'd learned on my own, the hard way. Above all, they validated my belief that being a good leader means developing your own leadership style based on your values and personality. Leadership books and seminars can help you discover your leadership style, but to be a true leader it must come from within.

In other words, don't try to be somebody else. Always hold true to your core beliefs and do the right thing based on your character.

The Ladder Crumbles

After a few weeks, I started looking for another job, never imagining how hard it would be. I was staying in the same industry and was constantly being told I was over qualified. I never understood this because I never made it to an interview to discuss salary or position.

My application submission process became selective because I didn't want to get back into a situation where I didn't have the passion to do great work. It would have been hard for me to work for a competitor since I had spent so much time bidding against them.

As time went on, I began to realize I was in for a challenge. Hunting for a job was not a specialty of mine, and I hadn't had to do it in a very long time.

After four or five months, which seemed like an eternity, a friend I had worked with referred me to a physician recruitment company that was looking for a telemarketer. I didn't know anything about the business, but it was a job and I could no longer stand not working.

Taking a seventy percent pay cut to work in a field I wasn't comfortable in and that didn't fit my skills was devastating. Like my dad, I took this job out of necessity, not because I wanted to.

My new boss tried to help me, and even created a fancy position with a big title to encourage me, but he knew I wasn't happy. The work wasn't for me. It required a lot of phone conversations to set up meetings and sell a service I was unfamiliar with. I was a face-to-face relationship guy. I was meeting my quotas, but I was back to where I dreaded the drive to work. I gave my all to the job for the eight hours I was there, but I just didn't have much extra to offer being so much out of my element.

It was a small company that hadn't done any marketing. I didn't understand the industry, but I set up a website and introduced them to a few contacts. I helped them understand a different perspective on marketing and managing employees. My boss was a salesman trying to run a business. He clearly thought all people thought like him and could sell like he did. I became more of an advisor than telemarketer.

One day, he told me something that sounded oddly familiar: "You're better than this. Do you want to do something different?"

He could just as easily have let me go, but instead he offered to partner with me in a new venture. He asked me to come up with an idea, write a business plan, and pick a business name. We'd be fifty-fifty partners. He also told me he'd bankroll the business with $50,000. I suppose I should have been more excited about this offer — it's not every day that someone offers you $50,000 to start your own business. But it didn't feel right—it felt too good to be true. Maybe I was more shocked than excited at the time. More likely it was that the most basic of business concepts—relationship—was missing. We had not had the time to build a true relationship.

I felt like I was back in my lawn cutting days. Although I'd been around business for a while, and even launched Advantage Computers on my own, I really didn't understand what a business plan entailed. Advantage had been more of a hobby that I hoped would make money. I had no earthly idea what kind of business I could start. Besides, how could I run a business? I wasn't a businessman. I wasn't educated in business. If I'd had a list of the top one hundred things I wanted to do in life at that time, starting and running a business wouldn't have been one of them.

Yes, I had goals in life, desiring to take care of my family. Starting a company wasn't one of them. I was a bit of a risk taker though, so why not use that to start a business?

I have a bit of an addictive personality, and gambling added an edge for me. It was never about the money— most of my bets were for a single dollar—but I'd bet just about anyone anything. "I'll bet you a dollar" was something I said a lot, and I played the lottery every week on the chance that I might get lucky. I honestly thought at one time that playing the lottery and gambling was how I was going to secure my family's financial goals.

I wasn't afraid to step out there. Risk had never bothered me. In fact, I thrived on it. Owning a business seemed beyond my knowledge base. Other than my lawn care company as a teen, I had no business education or experience running a formal company. In the back of my mind, maybe I always questioned whether I'd make it with the company.

The benefit of a willingness to take risks is that it allows you to step out. To be a leader you must be out front, and willing to step into the darkness. If something felt right, I didn't hesitate, and this part of my personality would serve me well in my coming venture.

Why Can't I?

I started looking at people who owned their own businesses and began to ask myself why I couldn't do that, too. After all, I'd sort of done it when I was a kid, and I'd made a success of it.

> *You must believe in yourself before others will follow you.*

The next week, I sat down and wrote a so-called business plan focusing on what I knew. The problem was, all I knew was the health care equipment service business, and I wasn't sure I wanted to do that anymore. Maybe I wanted something different. I thought about the car business since that was Brenda's background. She was quick to tell me I didn't want to do that. I'm not sure she wanted me to work with her. Truthfully, she knew the car sales business was tough, and at times, cutthroat. That's not me and she knew it.

Maybe consulting in the industry I knew so well was a better fit for me. Perhaps advising others on how to do what I felt I was so good at could benefit them. I had been involved in the outsourcing of services for most of my career. Maybe I could help hospitals in-source, help them set up their own service program, and save money from outsourcing.

For the last twelve years, I worked as an outsourced option for hospitals, convincing them outsourcing was their best option to save money. I knew all the sales pitches, the disadvantages of running their own programs, and the advantages to outsourcing. If I could take all that knowledge and apply it to help them compete against outsourced options, I could show them higher savings. What possible reason could they have for saying no? The concept sounded great on paper.

Given my struggles with writing, I felt I needed someone I trusted to read my business plan and give me an honest opinion before presenting it to my boss. I liked and respected Brenda's boss, so I asked him to read it over the weekend and give me some feedback. He was a lot like I wanted to be: he treated his people well, everyone liked working for him, and he'd successfully built a number of car dealerships.

I was anxious and nervous when I arrived at his office early Monday morning to talk with him. To this day, I remember sitting in a chair, my palms sweating, and waiting for his response.

"Son, do you believe in this?" Those were his first words.

I replied, "Yes, sir; I believe it will work."

He immediately reached into his desk, pulled out a checkbook, and wrote me a check to fund the start-up of the company. It was a lot of money, or at least that's what I thought at the time. I was certain $30,000 would go a long way, but I quickly learned that's not the case when setting up a business.

He said, "Here's a lesson, son: if it's something you truly believe in, you don't need partners. Hard work, dedication, passion, and a don't-give-up attitude will get you there."

I told him I couldn't pay him back, and he told me he expected nothing in return.

I walked out of his office in complete shock and showed the check to Brenda, who was equally amazed.

Looking back, maybe we shouldn't have been as surprised as we were. Brenda was one of his most trusted employees. She had helped him set up multiple dealerships and oversaw all his business assets.

Still, even though I knew I had to make a change of some kind, I wasn't sure I should actually accept the check. Brenda and I never wanted to owe anyone money. Being in debt or taking advantage of someone was not something we ever wanted to do.

On the other hand, my current job was not for me. I was miserable driving to work every day, and I'm sure it showed. What's more, even though Brenda was making a nice salary, money was running low in our household, and pressure was running high.

Brenda never handled our personal finances. She had her own money and paid for the kids' babysitting and daycare and her "fun" expenses. I had drawn out my 401(k) to pay living expenses and was managing credit cards to pay credit cards. I was doing whatever I needed to keep supporting my family. I was the man of the house and it was my responsibility to take care of them.

Brice was eight and Braden was only two years old. I never wanted them to think their dad couldn't provide everything they wanted or needed. My goal was to always make my family proud.

After some discussion, Brenda and I reluctantly decided to take the money. I'd start a new company and use everything I'd ever learned to run it. We were confident we could make it as long as she continued to work while I built the new company.

We also committed to returning the money to him multifold, because we didn't want to take advantage of his generosity. To be honest, I don't think Brenda cared much what I did, as long as we didn't let her boss down.

At work the next morning, my boss asked about my business plan. I thanked him but surprised him by turning in my resignation and declining his offer for $50,000. As grateful as I was, he wasn't familiar with the business I was proposing nor did he know me. Why would he want to invest in me?

I decided to take the advice I'd received from Brenda's boss to never form a partnership with someone who doesn't bring equal or greater value to the relationship.

I know I couldn't have been the best of company during this time. I hadn't been happy in my work for quite a while, and for the past year, wasn't able to support my family as I'd been accustomed to doing. If I ever let my guard down or displayed a hint of stress, Brenda would feel it and the stress would multiply.

Things would get worse before they got better, but the risk I was about to take would position us for better things down the road.

CHAPTER 9

Stepping Off the Ledge in More Ways Than One

The next chapter of life was about to begin. In part, this was because once again someone believed in me and encouraged me to believe in myself.

More importantly, I was willing to embrace Principle 4—Pursue It—and chase after my dreams, or to put it a more sobering way, risk it all.

On March 1, 1999, a new member of our family was born, our business. Little did we know at the time, but CREST Services would become one of the fiercest competitors in the entire medical equipment service industry.

> *You can't win if you don't play! Sometimes you need to take the risk.*

I loved the name CREST, but to legally incorporate a name it must be different than other incorporated names. My attorney suggested we could use CREST Services as a "doing business as" (DBA), but we needed a legal name to incorporate. This basically meant we would be doing business as CREST Services no matter the legal business name. My creativity kicked in and I came up with the legal name, Clinical Resources for Equipment Support Technology Services, Inc. I regretted this later as I could have used any legal name and still used CREST Services. Can you imagine writing that full legal name on every credit application, contract, and official corporate document?

We began as a consulting company working with hospitals—just like I'd written in my business plan. We would help them in-source their medical equipment services. In other words, we would help them set up their program, recruit the personnel, train the new employees on the program, and continually support them with backup service and parts for their medical equipment service needs. This was the work I'd specialized in since the day I'd first put on a tie back in 1985.

Everything I believed in, everything I'd ever learned, everything I stood for was about to be tested. I was stepping off the ledge, and it was my first big leap into the great unknown.

Stand by your principles, no matter what you face.

I started with a few basic principles. The most important was to treat my employees, vendors, and customers with the highest level of respect, with no one individual having more importance than any other.

If the first rule about business is "It's all about relationships," the old adage "It's not what you know, it's who you know" was about to be tested.

Wanting to go big, I set up the corporation, established a mailing address, set up a home office with a dedicated phone number, developed a corporate logo and some sales material, and was ready to grow.

Of course, I did all this with the help of some very important relationships I'd built and some trusted advisors, including referrals to an attorney and a CPA from the car dealership where Brenda worked.

That CPA has been our CPA since day one and is still one of Brenda's and my most trusted advisors today. That speaks to the strength of the relationships we were building.

Within a few weeks, we were in business, at least in theory if not in practice.

Relationships...Don't Burn 'Em or Abuse 'Em

I spent the first few months reaching out to old contacts and sending out mailings. Working from home, I learned to do web design to save costs on setting up our website. I began writing operational policies so we would be ready when the calls started coming in. I spent most days just waiting for the phone to ring, sometimes wandering out to the front yard to shoot hoops, looking for some stress relief while waiting for "the call."

I remember one particular call from a friend asking if I could meet him for lunch in Dallas. I told Brenda I was going and she responded as a true realist: "Why are you going? All he really wants is a free meal." I went anyway, hoping it might lead to business, all the while knowing I couldn't afford it and stressing over the cost of that twenty-dollar meal.

It was a major struggle to stay focused. My business model targeted big hospitals, but I was getting a lot of calls for hourly work with smaller clinics. I feared that if I chased the money on those smaller jobs, I wouldn't have the opportunity or time to focus on my target market.

Then I got a call from another old friend asking me to come to San Antonio to talk about potential business. Air travel, a hotel, and unnecessary expenses were out of the question, so I drove the six hours down and six hours back for an hour and a half meeting. These were things I had to do to save money and build relationships. This led to several new introductions. The meeting served more as motivation than as a true sales call for a prospective customer as it turned out. Meetings such as these took place many times. Whenever I needed to hear a positive voice from time to time, I'd call on several of my past relationships for words of encouragement. At times, this became a daily event.

One day, one of those calls turned into a new relationship. It was one of those "friend of a friend" calls. She had begun her own business and was struggling like I was to get it started. We were in hospital service for different-but-related departments, so we shared contacts. One of those contacts led to an introduction to a key hospital director in Houston.

I met with the potential customer to help him interview a possible employee to manage his program. Afterward he asked if CREST could provide the service directly. He proposed that we hire the technician and set up the program ourselves. He trusted me without a doubt because of his trust in the person who had introduced us.

Even though this didn't fit within the business model, I jumped at the chance out of sheer desperation. Our personal finances were dwindling after several months of no salary. I didn't want to implement full-service programs or have a lot of employees, but I had to get money coming into the company.

This was the first of many adjustments to the service model I had established for the company. I prided myself on being flexible, and since I was desperate for work, I changed the model. I would fit into the customer's box, not try to make the customer fit into mine. In other words, I would give customers what they wanted and needed, not what I wanted them to have.

It all paid off in October of 1999 when that customer signed a three-year deal for CREST to provide full-service support to their two Houston hospitals. The contract required that CREST provide two full-time employees to work on-site at the hospitals. The agreement also included two hospitals in Los Angeles, California. Fortunately, those hospitals sold prior to us taking them over. This was a good thing since we were already scrambling to get our policies in place and equipment purchased to handle the two Houston facilities. Two more would have been too much for CREST to manage successfully.

The contract came none too soon. With two boys to support, a house payment to make, and my new venture anything but a sure success, life was stressful. Brenda and I no longer had time to enjoy each other. We focused on the boys and our own personal concerns, but I was all too aware that since I'd stopped working, we had accumulated considerable debt and spent our retirement money.

One of the most stressful days of my life was telling Brenda that we were out of money and had to sell our house. She was supportive but also surprised. We didn't discuss personal finances. She preferred to not worry about it and just let me handle it. I didn't want to stress her out, so I handled it.

Honestly, I was afraid to let her know how bad it was. She considered herself a realist and I was afraid if I told her she would tell me to "quit the business and go get a job." I didn't want to hear that, so I didn't give her the opportunity to say it.

The weekend before the three-year deal was official, we actually went to look at a rental home. The signed contract came in just days before we put our house on the market.

We decided to hold off on selling our home and just wait and see what would happen. I was certain if I focused on doing a great job for my new customers, CREST would grow. We lived in the Dallas area, so managing a new customer account based in Houston could be a challenge. I believed everything would go smoothly if I simply focused on my core values and delivered what was promised.

Things were beginning to look up.

A Whole New World

Initially, I envisioned that CREST would become a consulting company, not to exceed a few employees, with business revenue just under $1 million. We were going to help hospitals transition outsourced programs back to their internal employees, and then recruit, train, and support them. Not only did that first customer change our business model, it quickly revealed how much I didn't know about running a business.

> Think outside the box. You never know where the solution will come from.

I was never involved in the financials of my previous company, so my experience was limited to bidding contracts. In other words, I never knew if my bids actually generated profits. Likewise, I had never been in charge of payroll, or payables, or receivables, or billing, or cash base, or accrual based accounting, or P&L reporting, or sales tax, or, or, or...

I went back to what I'd learned about using outside vendors to support services in a hospital. Once I accepted the fact that I couldn't do everything internally, I contracted with an outside staffing and human resources firm to give our company the image of a well-established corporation with full benefits. This was always intended as a temporary solution, with plans to bring it in-house as soon as possible.

I decided to focus on what I did best and trust others to fill the gaps. If this endeavor was to be successful, I had to accept that I didn't know it all and needed assistance. This required determining where to focus my attention in the new company. I knew it had to be on finding business or there wasn't going to be a company to build. However, if I spent all my time doing the actual work, there would be no future growth. Trying to balance growth and operations and financials led to many sleepless nights filled with excitement, nervousness, happiness, stress, anxiety, joy, and sadness. It was an emotional roller coaster ride, to say the least.

In order to support this new contract and provide the full on-site service it would require, I decided to hire a close friend with excellent customer service skills and the ability run a program, who wanted to be part of a dream, and was willing to travel. Given his knowledge, I had no worries about him starting up the Houston account. Once he was put into position, I was free to handle operations and continue to build the business from Dallas.

Now that we had employees, there were payroll and benefits and travel expenses to worry about, and I wasn't even on the payroll yet. It may not be a well-known fact, but when you start a new business, the first person to not get paid is you. Even so, we managed a tight budget by eating cheap meals and staying in some pretty sketchy hotels.

Nonetheless, we must have been doing something right, because for Christmas 1999, our first holiday party, our client gave us their limousine and driver to use for the night. They told us we were doing great work. We were to go out and enjoy ourselves, so we drove around looking at Christmas lights and then stopped for dinner at Benihana.

In our first twelve months of business, we had five employees, signed contracts with four hospitals and booked $745,000 in revenue. That twenty-dollar meal I struggled to pay for led to signing the fourth hospital in late 1999.

Best of all, we were making our customers happy and I was still wearing a tie.

Don't Let Anything Get in the Way

The year 2000 started with a bang. This was appropriate, given that Y2K was likewise expected to begin with a bang; there were a lot of concerns about medical equipment and how the Y2K issue would affect services.

Late in 1999, we had signed our first large hospital in the Dallas area. I spent that New Year's Eve at our new customer's site, side by side with all the hospital executives. Thankfully, Y2K actually caused no more than a small ripple and it was a quiet night.

I didn't know it at the time, but that hospital CEO was friends with another CEO in Arizona, one whose hospital was part of a much larger health care organization. The CEO in Dallas was impressed with the work we were doing and mentioned us to his friend.

After being referred to this hospital, we expanded into Arizona and then New Mexico. We subsequently broke the $1 million gross revenue mark — our target revenue goal from inception — and finished the year 2000 with ten employees.

I began our first advertising campaign, but not for new business. Instead, we advertised for employees. Through trade journals and trade shows, I began building our brand. These industry advertisements set the stage for us to become a national provider people wanted to work with. We were seen as a small company on the rise, and

I continued building CREST through employee networking and references.

The friend I visited with in San Antonio the year before had left his position with the hospital there and started a company recruiting talent in our industry. We partnered to recruit top talent for our organization, with military veterans as our primary candidates. It was a win-win relationship—his business was growing while he helped us grow.

From 2002 to 2003, revenue increased from $2.5 to $4.1 million entirely through the relationships we built during our first year. I signed a five-year lease on our first official corporate office to begin in June of 2003. But life had other plans.

Pain, Pain Go Away

In late April of that year, I started having severe back pains and began losing weight. I was traveling a lot and had been on a diet, so I didn't think anything was wrong. I was actually happy to be losing weight, but by the first week of May I was losing two pounds per day and experiencing tremendous pain in both calves.

After a visit to one of our accounts outside of Philadelphia, I was so sore I barely managed to catch the flight home.

Within five days, I was unable to stand. Our closest friend insisted I see a doctor because she was tired of hearing me complain.

I was reluctant to go because I thought I just had sore muscles that would go away in time. Needless to say, I never expected what was to come.

Laugh and smile. It's contagious.

After my initial visit, the doctor lined up tests. Monday was blood work, Tuesday we redid the blood work, Wednesday was a CAT scan, and on Thursday, I was admitted to the hospital. A lot of what happened is a blur, but I went through test after test. They did nuclear medicine studies, CTs, and MRIs, and poked and prodded me all over. My doctors suspected I had an infectious disease, but I hadn't been anywhere to contract one.

I was lying in the MRI machine when the doctor came in and asked if I could handle another scan. I had a feeling he'd finally seen something, and after almost two weeks of tests, I was more than ready to know what was going on.

Shortly after I returned to my room, my doctor came in and announced he'd found a tumor.

Great! Finally, we had an answer.

The doctor informed us it was located in my lower lumbar spine among bundles of nerves. It was considered inoperable.

Okay, what could we do?

He wanted to perform a biopsy and then try to treat the tumor.

Great! A plan!

Brenda sat in the corner speechless, teary eyed, and in total shock. Outwardly, I was trying to be strong, but inside I was a mess. I was ready for just about anything to get rid of this severe pain.

The doctors made several unsuccessful attempts to biopsy the tumor using non-surgical methods. After a few days, my doctor decided it would be necessary to schedule a surgical biopsy.

Keep a "glass is half full," optimistic outlook.

The neurologist's main hospital where he performed surgery was not where I was admitted originally, so I had to move hospitals for the biopsy. The neurologist was one of many doctors trying to find what was wrong with me. I was assigned an oncologist, neurologist, nephrologist, a generalist, and probably a few other "ologists" I didn't even know about.

It's a small world. Upon meeting my nurse at the new hospital and engaging in general conversation about what I did for a living, I found out she was the girlfriend of one of my former coworkers in East Texas. Sure enough, I immediately began receiving a touch of extra care, reminding me again of how important it is to treat everyone you meet with respect—you never know who you might be talking to or how you'll meet up again.

A quick thirty- to forty-five-minute surgery was planned to biopsy the tumor in my spine to determine the best treatment path. Brenda was holding my hand as they rolled me out of the room and headed toward surgery. She gave me a quick kiss on the cheek and I said, "See you in a few minutes." The last thing I remember before going under is lying on the operating table and wondering if I'd ever come back out. This was probably the first time I'd thought about not making it through this.

The last few minutes before the anesthesia kicked in, my mind raced as I thought about my wife, my kids, my parents, my friends, the company, and the possibility that I might never see any of them again. Although I was known for my eternally optimistic attitude and always wore a smile, I feared my time might be up.

When I awakened in recovery and saw the clock on the wall, I asked why it was so late. To my surprise, I learned I'd been in surgery for over six hours.

What had happened to thirty to forty-five minutes? Why did I have this catheter in place, and why was there an IV in my big toe?

Then I saw Brenda sitting next to me. She had not and would not leave my side. She looked horrible and beautiful at the same time. The stress of waiting during that interminable surgery must have been horrendous for her. But for the first time in a long time, I didn't feel any pain in my calves or back.

Brenda and the doctors told me that after discovering the nerve endings leading to my calves had all banded around the tumor, they'd taken a chance and made the decision to try to remove the entire thing, even at the risk of leaving me paralyzed.

They'd been successful in removing the tumor without any further damage to the spine or nerves, and though the jury was still out on the tumor itself, I savored the profound relief of being pain free.

Ready for Recovery

Post-surgery, I felt much better and couldn't wait to

leave the hospital and go home. It was Memorial Day weekend, and I was chomping at the bit. We were just waiting on the results of the biopsy and maybe some follow-up treatment.

You know that feeling you get when things perhaps aren't quite as positive as you'd hoped?

My nurses and primary care doctor seemed to be acting a little funny, and I had the vague feeling that something was wrong. I couldn't put a finger on it, but something was up.

When my oncologist came by early in the afternoon instead of at his normal time between ten and eleven at night, I again had the feeling that something was going on. Friends were visiting, and the doctor was using his best bedside manner, but I could tell.

"Put it out there, doctor; don't sugarcoat it," I said.

I still recall the next few moments in slow motion.

He stood there emotionless but with concern on his face. I know he has to do this a lot, tell people bad news, but I truly felt his concern. My biopsy had come back, and the tumor was malignant. I had cancer. It was some type of non-Hodgkin's lymphoma, and my blood was also infected due to a rare blood disorder related to acute leukemia.

"Acute" and "leukemia" in the same sentence didn't sound good, but still, no biggie, right? We just needed a plan.

Then our best friend asked the infamous question, "What stage is it?"

Although I'd never dealt with cancer before, the doctor's response left no doubt that I was in trouble.

"He's considered late stage four."

We asked about treatment options, and the doctor replied that there was no known treatment for this diagnosis. He estimated that I had about six months to live.

All I could do was look at Brenda, tears streaming down her cheeks, her hands trembling. I reached out to hold one, wrapping my hand gently around her fingertips. Our friend sat there and said, "Why not me? It should have been me." I didn't understand her comment, but it stuck with me.

I thanked the doctor and looked at our friend and said, "Please go get me a hamburger steak dinner with ketchup. I'm going to need all the energy I can get, because we are going to fight this."

Your attitude is important—and it's one of the few things you truly have control over. Choose it wisely.

CHAPTER 10

Taking the Bull by the Horns

There was no fixed plan for my treatment because my cancer was so rare and so advanced. The doctor said if I wanted to fight, he would develop a regimen.

The alternative was to go home and manage the pain until I died, but I was only thirty-eight years old. Why would I go home and die? I wasn't in any pain, and at this point, I didn't look or even feel sick.

> Don't let a challenge get you down. The bigger the challenge, the bigger the opportunity.

Nonetheless, a PET scan revealed that the cancer had spread throughout my body. A bone marrow biopsy was unsuccessful because I didn't have enough marrow left to draw due to the advanced stage of the cancer.

We learned that the leukemia had been with me for a while and that the tumor had basically prompted its discovery. In fact, if it hadn't been for the tumor, I likely would have died very soon with no explanation.

Looking back, the blood disorder made sense. I'd bruised easily my whole life (my nickname playing football in high school was "Bruiser"). I was chronically tired, I'd started having night sweats, and of course, I'd inexplicably begun losing weight.

That Saturday morning, instead of going home to start our holiday weekend, I went into surgery where I received my first chemo port. On Sunday morning, the first of many chemo bags was delivered.

This started a routine that lasted several months in which I received one drug after another after another, including chemo injections directly into my spine in two-week cycles. I was allowed to go home in between treatments as long my temperature stayed down. Without fail, as soon as I got home, my temperature would rise and I'd have to go back to the hospital. I was never home for more than one night, and about the time in each cycle when I began to feel better, it was time for another round.

Receiving the chemo bags wasn't painful; it was the after effects that did me in. Chemo is designed to kill the bad cells, but the good ones die right along with them. The different chemo drugs had different side effects, and reading all the drug information was overwhelming. I remember lying there watching my body be infused with chemicals knowing that within a couple days, I was going to be incredibly sick. From tingling fingers to the notoriously upset stomach, I experienced every possible side effect.

Worst of all, about every three weeks, I was taken into the radiation department, where methotrexate was injected directly into my spinal fluid. This didn't hurt or cause aftereffects, but I knew that if the technician missed the mark by even a fraction of an inch, I wouldn't be coming back, or at least not walking back. I always left my room telling Brenda, "See you in a few," but my smile only lasted until I left the room.

I could read the concern and stress on her face and always hoped my smile would help. I'm sure she felt like I did, that each and every time I left the room, I may not return. I made it back every time to see her sitting there waiting, happy to see me. I was always anxious to return, knowing she was waiting. She was there every single time.

My boys would only visit for short periods. I didn't like them seeing me this way, so sick, but I missed them dearly. I looked forward to their visits and did not want them to leave, but I also did not want this to be their memory of me. Fortunately, they both had great friends supporting them and keeping them busy.

My Best Hospital Outfit

Brenda told me that Brice's teacher had called. He would be receiving an award at his end-of-year school program. I had missed so many events before due to working. But I was determined I would never miss another one if I could help it. After one of my rounds of chemo, I asked my doctor for permission to leave the hospital to attend the end-of-the-year school program. He agreed.

I went, all decked out in a hospital mask and sweats. I was a proud dad to hear his name get called and watch him cross the stage. I received some stares and strange looks, but I didn't care; I was there to enjoy every minute of being a proud father. It was a lesson I wished I had learned much earlier: never take these simple family moments for granted.

I was supposed to go straight back to the hospital, but on the way back, I told Brenda I wanted to go to the new office. I hadn't even seen it since we'd moved in!

Once we arrived, I sat in my office for about ten minutes, amazed and sad. Seeing my employees and the joy and concern on their faces was hard, and I hated leaving to go back to the hospital. I honestly didn't think I'd ever sit in that chair again.

My Last Will and Testament

I had lain on my hospital bed a few weeks before with my attorney and transcriptionist present writing my Last Will and Testament. We needed to deal with this. Brenda didn't like discussing the possibility of my death, but it was time to address the reality. The company and my family had to be taken care of.

CREST had some great people who cared about me and the future of the company. Many stepped up beyond my wildest dreams. The daily visits I received from key team members and the calls from employees were the highlights of my day.

One visit I remember clearly. Whenever I was able, we would go down to the hospital lobby to meet and talk with visitors. It was nice to get out of the room.

This had to be a scary sight for a hospital CEO. People in ties, meeting with a man in a hospital gown with an IV pole. One morning my nurse came in, laughing. She said they had received a call from administration asking who I was and why I was meeting with some professional people in the lobby. I actually got a short visit from the CEO after that. He laughed about it with me, but said, "You have to imagine where my thoughts were."

Brenda and I needed help at home, too. Brice and Braden, then twelve and five years old, moved to Mississippi with Brenda's parents for the summer. That fall, their grandparents moved to our home for the duration of the school year. Brenda's parents were retired and still in fairly good health so this made it much easier.

My parents were getting old and not in the best of health. My mother was diabetic and dealing with the onset of dementia. They would do their best, but had a hard time seeing their son so sick.

They only came to visit me one time while I was in the hospital. It was not a pleasant time for Brenda. My dad stayed at the hospital the whole time only talking about leaving his cats behind and how he needed to go back home to check on them. My mom seemed lost and didn't know what to do.

Brenda was upset with them for seemingly not caring about me and only being concerned about their pets back home. Nothing could have been further from the

> **Show empathy in life and in business. It's one of the most important traits you can develop.**

truth. My parents loved me dearly and, because I was good at empathy, I knew how they felt. Seeing me in that kind of shape was devastating for them. I overheard my dad say many times, "Parents are not supposed to outlive their children." Even though I was drugged and incoherent at times, I could still hear most everything.

I don't believe my dad knew how to deal with me in this shape. I was his baby, something he called me until the day he died.

My parents called daily and I could hear the concern in their voices. They didn't have to express their feelings. I knew. Brenda to this day remembers that visit and so do I; we just have different thoughts about it.

I'm not sure our boys ever fully understood what I was going through, but I know it was hard for them to see me this way. Brice was old enough to understand what was happening to some degree, but he showed no emotion. I think he was a lot like Brenda and just didn't want to deal with all this. Braden was too young to understand and was only told I had back issues.

A few years later, in his admissions essay to Texas A&M University, Brice wrote about how my diagnosis had impacted him. He talked about the moment he was told about his dad and how he sat there totally emotionless. He recalled one of his first jiujitsu matches where he hurt his thumb and told himself, "This is nothing compared to what my dad went through, so suck it up and get out there."

Until now, Brice had no idea I read his essay. Our neighbor, who had helped him edit it, called me and said, "You have to read this." She was almost crying when she handed it to me.

I have to admit, realizing how my cancer impacted him made me cry.

Sometimes the greatest lessons we get in our lifetimes aren't business lessons about making a profit, meeting budget or hitting benchmarks—they're about the *why*. One of the biggest lessons Brenda and I learned was the depth of our love for each other and our two sons. The distance that had crept in between us—from work and family demands—disappeared during our fight to beat my cancer. My love for my family has guided me and motivated me to climb higher.

They Looked So Real...

I could write a whole book about memorable things that occurred during my treatment, but a few stories stand out.

I was still handling payroll and some accounting functions for CREST when I was admitted to the hospital. I hired someone to take over the back office functions, but as a hands-on person, it was challenging for me to let go. I was in the process of training my new assistant when I was diagnosed.

You know those things you do that you know are wrong when you do them, but you just can't control yourself? I was supposed to approve payroll once it was entered—nothing more and nothing less. My assistant had completed all of the data entry and verification, but even during my cancer treatment I still was the only one with full approval rights. I approved payroll as she requested, but not until I'd paid many people extra for overtime, in some cases as much as ten thousand dollars extra! I guess I was feeling generous or maybe it was all the drugs. I handed the computer back to her with a smile.

Needless to say, that was the last payroll I've ever processed. Brenda and my assistant removed my authorization, so I promptly learned to let go of payroll. In fact, from that day forward that assistant became one of my most trusted employees, and more importantly, a great friend.

A few other stories stand out from my time in the hospital:

- Receiving a birthday card from my staff containing pictures of them goofing off at the office (they were a creative bunch).

- Undergoing my first chemo-related haircut. My hair had started falling out, so I'd asked an employee's wife to cut it for me. In the middle of the cut, I reached up and pulled a clump out. This kind of freaked everyone out, but I was on heavy medication and didn't know what I was doing.

- The pastor's wife's reaction when I answered her question regarding what I'd been doing all day (which is neither repeatable nor appropriate to include in this book).

- The "Look, no metal on me" show, a streaker flash, I gave the radiology technician before a scan. Since she was married to one of my employees, that was awkward.

- The beautiful waterfalls and antique furniture decorating my hospital room. I couldn't understand why no one else could see those beautiful blue waterfalls with the gleaming white sunshine behind them. Apparently they were hallucinations only visible to me, courtesy of the strong drugs I was on.

To this day, those images are as real as ever, and as horrible as this time was overall, these memories still make me smile.

CHAPTER 11

Time for a Bucket List

So many lengthy stays in the hospital left me with a lot of time on my hands. To help break up the monotony, Brenda brought me a laptop. With it, I began to research my dream home, my dream car, and where we would travel upon my release.

An unexpected benefit of my hospitalization was the chance for Brenda and I to get to know each other all over again. We played cards and games, watched movies for hours on end, and snuggled up in my hospital bed.

Up to this point in our lives, we traveled very little as a couple, and vacations had been nonexistent. With the decision to make up for lost time, we dreamed of trips using the Beach Boys' song "Kokomo" as inspiration. We decided Jamaica would be our first trip as soon as I could travel.

Brenda and I started writing a bucket list that included:

- Build a house on the beach.
- Put family first and have more adventures together.

- Take at least two trips a year, one with the family and one for just the two of us.

Though I couldn't build a house on the beach or travel quite yet, I could fulfill at least one of my personal wishes: buy my dream car. On one of my planned go-home days, Brenda asked if I wanted to go anywhere. I told her to take me to the Lexus dealership.

Bless her heart, she didn't try to discourage me, so off we went.

I remember walking in the door and asking for a SC430 hardtop convertible, black on black, and telling the salesman I needed to be out of there in thirty minutes.

The look on his face was priceless.

He turned to Brenda, and all she could do was smile and tell him to do what I'd asked.

About ten minutes later, he returned to say they didn't have one in stock, but the general manager had one and was willing to sell it.

Forty-five minutes later, we were driving off in a new SC430 hardtop convertible, black on black. I wanted to own a sports car at least once in my life. I figured this may be my only chance. Unfortunately, I was way too unstable to drive; my hands were always shaky and my reflexes were slow. But it was mine!

We kept that car less than a year. My chemo treatments had left me too sensitive to the sunlight to take it out for more than a few minutes during the day. After many bumps to the curb, Brenda stopped letting me drive anyway.

Later when I learned I might just live a few more years after all, I walked backed into that same dealership, met with the same salesman, and told him I needed to trade the convertible in—now that I was going to live, I couldn't afford it. Apparently, he didn't see the humor in my reasoning.

I purchased a Lexus from that dealership for years after that. Because of the relationship I built with the people there, I still call them today when I'm looking for a new car.

Winning the War

Obviously you know that I beat this cancer, or I wouldn't be writing a book years later. Let me tell you how I—or rather how we—did it.

Sometime around September of 2003, my doctor paid me a visit. After bluntly telling us, "Well, you've made it this far, which is longer than I expected," he said he wanted to refer me to a doctor who could offer additional treatment.

We were all in. We'd made it this far, so why stop now?

We were referred to a bone marrow transplant specialist at Medical City Dallas Hospital. I felt this was a good omen. I knew this hospital well—it was where I'd moved back into operations with my former company in 1994.

After meeting with the new doctor, we had a good feeling that this was how and where we wanted to continue treatment. I was put on the bone marrow transplant list after a few weeks of evaluation.

Being admitted to Medical City Dallas Hospital was quite an experience. Not only did it save my life, but it also greatly influenced the success of my company in the years that followed. Seeing the hospital from the patient's perspective and truly understanding its core business—patient care—gave me a firsthand understanding of the role support service plays.

Within a few weeks, I had two matches on the transplant list, and we began test after test after test. I had bone marrow biopsies, blood work, and scans every day, or so it seemed. There wasn't a lot of information available about bone marrow transplants in 2003, but I do remember one nurse describing what was about to happen: I would be taken to death's door, and just before the door closed, I would be brought back. I couldn't comprehend what that experience would be like. We had fought and come too far to turn around.

Turns out, her description was entirely accurate.

The week leading up to my planned transplant date was one of the hardest periods I've ever endured. It was a week of ultra-strong chemo and total body radiation, with the goal of destroying all my marrow and cancer cells and suppressing my immune system before replacing my bone marrow with the new marrow.

At that time (and possibly still today), when you underwent total body radiation, you were packed in a box with bags of rice to help ensure the radiation was distributed evenly. I called it a "casket." It seemed fitting.

Sitting in the casket of rice preparing for whole body radiation was an experience I will never forget. Each morning and afternoon, I rode a stretcher to and from the radiation room. Lying there totally surrounded and unable to move for an hour while they administered the treatment was almost unbearable at times, not because it hurt—the treatment was actually painless—but because it gave me time to focus on the reality that there was no turning back.

I remember when they finally allowed Brenda to come down and see me being packed in rice bags prior to my final treatment. She had to have felt as scared and isolated as I did. I tried to maintain a smile and positive attitude, but inside I was scared to death. I loved life, I loved Brenda, and I was grateful that we were growing closer again.

Visitations were limited due to my immune system being suppressed. For the week leading up to the transplant and the few weeks following, Brenda was the only person allowed to stay with me. She could not come and go and would have to scrub everything if she left the room and came back. We went for weeks not being able to see our boys.

I still don't know how she did it, but she never left my side.

My New Birthday

November 19, 2003 — transplant day — became my new birthday. The transplant process wasn't what we expected, but then again, we didn't know what to expect.

The nurse came in that morning with a bag of what looked like plasma. I'd had close to fifty blood transfusions by now, so honestly, it all looked the same to me.

My nurse explained that the plasma would be infused via my central line very slowly over the course of several hours. She would be there the entire time watching and taking my vitals.

It actually seemed anticlimactic at the time, but we knew the hard part was going to be the recovery process.

Sure enough, recovering from the bone marrow transplant was by far the hardest thing I've ever done. I don't remember much about the time right after the transplant. My body was weak and my mouth so messed up that I couldn't eat. The radiation had destroyed my mouth. My tongue was so damaged that layers would peel off at the slightest touch. Food was almost impossible to eat. I used special mouthwash to cleanse and numb my mouth. I would get up and try to brush my teeth every couple hours to get some relief. It was hard just to breathe. After all the pain and chemo effects, the mouth was now causing me unbearable agony.

Thanksgiving Day, less than ten days post-transplant, I awoke to see Brenda and the nurses standing over me. When I asked what was going on, they told me I'd stopped breathing. This occurred one other time while I was in the recovery phase, and to this day I still remember seeing a bright white light. All I can say is, since I'm still here, I guess there's a reason.

I remember lying in my hospital bed with Brenda, playing cards for hours on end. Yes, they allowed her to lay in bed with me, at least most of the nurses allowed it. They would warn us it wasn't good for us to be so close because of my decreased immune system. They would walk away knowing she was going to be right back in the bed. Most of them would just smile and look the other way.

I would walk with her around the circle on the hospital transplant floor several times a day. The transplant center was on the top floor of the hospital. It had twelve rooms with the nurses' station in the middle. I couldn't leave that floor but I could walk that circle. Each day, I would walk more circles, and I focused on the fact that the more I could walk, the sooner I could go home.

> *It sounds cliché until you've been there: enjoy today because tomorrow may never come.*

Being a goal-oriented person, I set other timelines in my head to help me reach this goal, including watching my blood count numbers climb. They would post my daily blood counts on the board; the numbers had to reach certain levels before I could go home. I would have to complete so many circles each day before I could go home. I would have to eat a certain amount before I could go home. I got in trouble for mashing my food so it would appear I had eaten more than I had. I wasn't fooling anyone.

I was getting my sense of humor back. Having knowledge of how to service a variety of medical equipment, I began to mess with the nurses. I would put the IV pump in service mode and cause it to do weird things. It drove the nurses crazy until they figured out what I was doing.

Funny thing about my industry, it's a fairly small world. The director of medical equipment service at the hospital was a former employee of that company where I had spent twelve years. They called him to come talk to me about messing with the equipment. We laughed about it and I promised not to do it again. He had taken over when I left that hospital in 1994 and eventually came to work for me at CREST.

During my chemo treatments, I'd often gone home only to end up back at the hospital the same day or later that night. I was determined that when I went home this time, I wouldn't be readmitted. I was willing to put in the extra time to be sure I could go home and stay home.

It worked. Once I checked out of Medical City, I was never readmitted, although Brenda and I made many trips to the clinic for checkups. I also returned to the hospital at least three times a week for tests and follow ups, more blood transfusions, and many supplemental blood count booster shots.

Bodies change after they undergo a transplant. They truly experience a rebirth. Sure enough, my DNA, blood type, and even my eating habits changed. What's more, thanks to my bone marrow transplant, I became a chimera. That means that my blood DNA is different than the rest of my cells. You may have seen this highlighted on an episode of the popular TV show, *CSI*. My blood DNA does not even match my kids. One thing I never expected (it probably wasn't important at the time): with my bone marrow transplant not only did I get a new birthday but I also had to get all my childhood vaccinations again!

To my surprise, I took on many traits of my donor. He liked dry cereal, and I began eating cereal out of the box, something I'd never done before. I used to love French fries, and now I couldn't stand them. Later, after we met him, I learned that he hated French fries, too.

The Million Dollar Diet

When I first thought about writing a book, I came up with a working title, *The Million Dollar Diet*. I chose this title somewhat facetiously, based on the cost of my treatment and the fact that I was about 255 pounds when I began feeling sick but by the time I left the hospital eight months later, I weighed 150 pounds.

> You're writing your own story every day of your life—be aware of what you're putting into it.

I remember Brenda and our friend sitting on the floor with all the insurance paperwork and hospital bills laid out while they tried to figure how we were going to pay them. The total amount for 2003 was somewhere around $980,000. Fortunately, we had great insurance, which paid a large portion of the costs. We still had to cover co-pays and deductibles.

Looking back, even though I progressed fairly well, this was still a terrible time. I'm ashamed to admit it, but my attitude was often lousy, and I deeply regret how I treated my wife during this period. My body was tired, my mind was drained, and though my fight had been fought and won, I felt I'd reached my capacity.

As a risk taker, I wasn't familiar with fear of anything. I didn't want to die. At times, I wanted to walk outside the room and scream.

I never asked, "Why me?" regarding the cancer. I wouldn't wish my experience on anyone. I accepted it but wouldn't let it kill me. I never was angry about my diagnosis of cancer. I was determined to come out of it a stronger, better man.

They say you lash out at the ones you love most and yes, it's true. Since Brenda was always there, she saw the moments when I couldn't take the excruciating pain any more.

Friends and other family would come and go, but Brenda remained. I struggled maintaining my demeanor twenty-four hours a day. Between the cancer and the treatments, the company and the employees, financials and the bills, my boys and the family, there were times it was too much. I can never express the sorrow I feel for the way I treated the one I love most, the person who left me only one night during the entire eight months of inpatient care and accompanied me on countless trips to the doctor.

I saved her life in 1987, and she saved mine in 2003.

CHAPTER 12

Unselfish Giving

Sometime during the first year post-transplant, I was asked if I would like to meet my donor. Of course my answer was yes, and I soon learned that my donor had also consented to meet me.

We were excited to meet and requested to set it up immediately. We found out we must wait a year. We wondered why. This didn't make sense to us. We were told that strict confidentiality standards protecting the privacy of the patient and the marrow donor are followed by the National Marrow Donor Program (NMDP), which operates the Be The Match Registry.

In 2003, the odds were not great for surviving a bone marrow transplant. Not so much due to the transplant itself, but the danger from having a non-existent immune system. You were more likely to die of the flu or pneumonia than from rejecting the transplant. We knew deep down this was the real reason for the waiting period.

During one of my regular trips to the clinic, the transplant coordinator gave Brenda and me some exciting news: my donor and I had been selected to represent bone marrow recipients at the area bone marrow society's annual meeting in Fort Worth. My donor and I would meet for the first time that evening at the banquet.

I could only invite three other people with a guest. In addition to our sons and Brenda's mom, we invited my doctor and a nurse's aide whose smile and positive attitude were so uplifting that we referred to her as "Very Lovely." My parents were not able to make the trip. I do regret them not being part of it. Maybe this would have given them more hope that I was getting better.

When we arrived at the banquet, our family was put in a small room and told to wait. I was nervous about meeting the man who had saved my life by selflessly donating his bone marrow, but when he and his wife walked in, we immediately connected. We exchanged gifts and hugs and learned a little about them. After a short visit, the banquet team told us that in about an hour, we would be introduced on stage and we should act surprised, as if this were our first meeting.

Unselfish giving is the best gift you will receive.

I don't think I ever saw someone smile as much as that nurse's aide at our table, reminding us again how she earned her nickname. I believe as much as she had affected me, I had affected her. There we all sat in that banquet room with my doctor and his wife, my nurse's aide and her husband, my family, and all the local government officials and staff of the local bone marrow association. When the mayor of Fort Worth introduced my donor and me, it wasn't hard to act surprised. The emotions flowed all over again. I even saw my doctor's smile and a bit of a tear in his eye.

To this day, my donor and I still talk and exchange Christmas gifts, and it was a great pleasure to celebrate my (second) tenth birthday with him and his wife in Las Vegas in 2013.

Be A Donor...It's the Right Thing to Do

It's my book, so I can't resist encouraging you to consider being a donor. It's quick and easy to sign up, and as I can testify, it saves lives.

When I first met my donor, I found out he'd only been on the list for seven days. He signed up through a drive at his office organized by Be The Match on behalf of a friend's daughter and was told the odds of ever being called were very low.

Seven days later, I came along.

I took the following description of Be The Match from their website at www.bethematch.org:

For the thousands of people diagnosed every year with life-threatening blood cancers like leukemia and lymphoma, a cure exists. Over the past 25 years, Be The Match ®, operated by the National Marrow Donor Program® (NMDP), has managed the largest and most diverse marrow registry in the world. We work every day to save lives through transplant.

By joining the registry, you are taking the first step to being the cure for patients with blood cancers like leukemia and other marrow diseases. It is also a commitment that you will take the next step if a patient needs you to donate your cells for a life-saving bone marrow transplant.

Joining the registry requires a sample of cells, usually collected by swabbing the inside of your cheek. This sample is used to compare specific protein markers, known as human leukocyte antigens (HLA), with HLA markers of patients who need a bone marrow transplant.

Doctors search the Be The Match Registry® to find donors with HLA markers that match those of their patients. These searches happen on behalf of patients every day, so the most important thing registry members can do is stay committed.

When a registry member matches a patient, there are several steps before the donation actually occurs. These steps are meant to ensure donation is safe for both the donor and the patient.

Being a donor is safe and saves lives, so please consider signing up.

A Welcome Recovery

I can't identify exactly when I recovered or was officially considered to be in remission, but I celebrated many milestones along the way.

I was thirty-eight when I was diagnosed with cancer and thirty-nine when I received the bone marrow transplant.

The first occasion I celebrated was the one-year mark post-transplant, and boy, did we celebrate. I had survived a full year!

Three years post-transplant was when I started feeling noticeably better.

By five years, I felt fully recovered.

At ten years, I was ready to celebrate.

I set a goal to retire when I turned fifty years old. That would be year twelve. I wanted to enjoy the fruits of my labor with my family and friends, assuming I did in fact live that long.

> Goals aren't just for big corporations. What do you want to achieve? Set your goals and go after them.

I was told that by age fifty I could expect to feel like I was sixty-five. Thanks to the effects of the numerous chemo and radiation treatments, problems such as cataracts, constant body and bone aches, and muscle tone issues would become apparent.

I was diagnosed with osteopenia in year two. Osteopenia refers to bone density that is lower than normal peak density but not low enough to be classified as osteoporosis. My mother had osteoporosis, so I knew the effects of it. I figured this was the first of many issues to come.

Not surprisingly, this prognosis became an important part of my personal and professional goals and objectives. Professionally, I was anxious to get back into the business and regain some sense of normalcy. Spending close to nine months inside the hospital and many more months making trips back and forth to the clinic seemed never-ending. Medications and a low immune system post-transplant didn't allow me to return to work full time for quite a while.

I was still receiving blood transfusions and injections to stimulate my blood counts. I don't remember exactly how long it was before I worked a full day, but even an hour here and there made me feel better. I was kept informed by my staff almost daily. They had done a great job holding things together.

The last business trip I took before being admitted to the hospital had been to one of our customers near Philadelphia, so it made sense that my first doctor-approved business trip would be back to see this same customer.

It took some talking, but I finally convinced the doctor to let me get on the plane after I agreed to the following conditions: the flight had to be less than three hours because of the lack of air circulation; I couldn't go alone; and I had to wear protective gear including a mask and gloves to protect me from potential germs in the air, since the treatments had so diminished my immune system.

A trusted friend and coworker agreed to go with me. The trip from Dallas to Philadelphia was flawless — I traveled all decked out in my mask and gloves, and though I received a few curious stares, I didn't mind in the least. I was on my way back to what I loved: getting to see my employees and them getting to see me. I think it was as important for them to see me back out as it was for me to be out.

Word spread fast that Brian was back. I used to play a game when I traveled, never telling anyone where I was or where I was going. It became known as "Where's Brian?" It would spread like wildfire on our instant message service and our internal discussion boards. When word got out that "The Game" was back on, it inspired me to get better and back to visiting.

I loved surprising my people. They would get creative in their efforts to try to figure out where I was. My assistant would even get calls asking, "What time am I supposed to pick up Brian?" to see if they could trick her into divulging my plans. Most of the time, Brenda was the only one who knew where I was going. It was as much fun for me as it was for them.

So, we made it to Pennsylvania and had a great visit with the staff there. Unfortunately, the trip back home wasn't quite as easy.

Once we were in the air, we found out a storm was hitting Dallas-Fort Worth and our flight would be diverted. After almost five hours in the air, we landed in Indianapolis, Indiana at one in the morning. Outwardly, I was all smiles and grateful to be off the plane. In all honesty, I was feeling worse by the minute.

Needless to say, my friend was stressed to the max. He just knew I was going to die mid-flight and that he'd be forced to face Brenda.

We finally checked in to the hotel, and I sent my friend to get a drink and bring me some Chick-fil-A, trying to assure him I was going to be okay.

I was okay, and thankfully, our flight home the next day was uneventful.

I'd taken the first step back to doing the work I loved.

Personally, Brenda and I were eager to get started on our bucket list before I was too frail to enjoy myself. Even with treatment, my doctor still only estimated another few months for me to live. Keeping his prognosis in mind, we looked at Jamaica. It was the first vacation site on our list, so we quickly arranged to travel with the friends who urged me to go to the doctor initially. I was so excited to finally start checking items off our list.

Despite being sick the entire flight, I did my best to hide it from Brenda to spare her the concern. Our renewed relationship was a huge blessing, but only compounded the loss she feared. Being together in Jamaica was euphoric. The sun, sand, and sea. It was just as we had dreamed: the view was postcard-perfect, the cool ocean breeze was blowing, and the warm sun was on our faces as we listened to the waves rolling in. This was it — our dream: live on the beach and enjoy every morning waking up to the sun shining and sounds of the waves rolling.

We treasured our time together there, and vowed to never take life for granted. Knowing tomorrow could be our last day, we were determined to live life to the fullest and enjoy every moment it had to offer.

It's amazing how it often takes a life or death crisis for many people to realize there's more to life than just work.

Surprise, Surprise

To celebrate my one-year birthday, Brenda suggested we attend a wine-tasting event. I couldn't drink alcohol just yet, but she's not normally one to plan things, so if she wanted to go somewhere, I was all in. We went to the Hilton DFW Lakes Executive Conference Center in Grapevine, a lovely hotel with beautiful ballrooms. We walked down the long hallway looking for the right room.

Actions always speak louder than words.

When I walked into the conference room, there stood all our friends and family, cheering.

I was dumbfounded. I was the planner. How had Brenda pulled this off without me knowing?

She'd invited well over 150 people whom I talked to on a regular basis, and many of them got up to speak (or in some cases tried to speak). Their words confirmed everything I've ever believed about how you can touch people without ever realizing it.

I was literally shaking as friends, colleagues, and family members got up and grabbed the microphone. It was all I could do to hold my emotions in check. Vendors I had worked with, customers I'd served, neighbors who had become friends, coworkers who were like family… each had a story about me and how I'd touched them.

My beautiful wife never said a word, and she didn't have to. I had seen the stress on her face and the wear and tear on her physically and emotionally. I saw the love in her eyes and the joy she radiated at still having me with her. We had survived the toughest year of our lives, and we had done it together. I wasn't the only cancer survivor in that room. The toll it had taken on her showed, but that night, nothing mattered but our love for one another.

When I look at pictures from that night, I still get emotional. It still stands as one of the greatest nights of my life.

CREST's Story and Our Story

When you are told you are dying at age thirty-eight and have less than six months to live but find yourself still alive two years later, you begin looking at your life and goals a little differently.

Brenda and I had our bucket list to complete, but even if I lived, I was expected to feel the devastating effects of my treatment by age fifty. In my mind, no matter how I sliced it, I only had a few good years left. I began to focus on how to build the business to give Brenda and I the freedom we wanted. The question became how could I balance a growing organization, work less, and enjoy life more. I'd taken baby steps toward letting go and trusting others, but now I needed to embrace this wholeheartedly.

Like many small business owners, I prided myself on being heavily involved in the day-to-day operations. In hindsight, it's amazing the company survived my absence, but our employees and their commitment to doing the right thing for our customers kept us in business. I later told those employees I couldn't have been more proud of how they'd filled the gap to keep CREST going.

By the end of 2003, in spite of my lengthy absence, we hit $4 million in revenue with business in more than ten states and thirty employees. All the philosophies I'd learned, believed in, and taught my employees had paid off. Nonetheless, 2003 was the only year our margins went down, and 2004 was the only year revenues didn't increase. It was clear it wasn't good for the company to be so dependent on me.

By late 2004, I felt better and was working more, and I was continuing to let go and let people do their jobs. It just wasn't possible to be involved in everything any longer. My mind seemed a bit slower than before, and I noticed that my memory, which was great pre-cancer, seemed to be fading. I had to rely on others more, so I focused on what I was best at, using my passion to chase new business and motivate employees, and enjoying my renewed relationship with Brenda.

I was coaching Braden's baseball team and attending more of Brice's school functions. I would reschedule my meetings to ensure I would not miss any more of my boys' events. In fact, I rescheduled a multi-million-dollar contract meeting so I would not miss Braden's baseball game. I moved an entire week of meetings to chaperone an orchestra trip to Boston with Brice. Oddly enough, these rescheduled meetings never affected my relationship with my customers. In fact, when I was honest and told them why I was rescheduling, it had the opposite effect.

Have passion for what you believe in!

Fortunately for CREST and for me, passion is something I've never lacked. Having a passion for what I did kept me smiling and put the "giddy up" in my step even through the toughest days. Training, motivating, and exciting people, always my strengths, soon became my exclusive focus.

My passion really showed when I was working with new personnel. I loved taking people who knew nothing about our industry, teaching them what they needed to know, and getting them excited. My love for training had begun early in my career when I'd helped develop a training program for new employees, and now this passion evolved into a love of teaching leadership skills to prospective leaders. I felt I was finally at Level 5 of Jim Collins' leadership pyramid where teaching others was more important than doing the actual work or supervising my team.

In 2004, our health insurance rates maxed out due to the costs of my cancer the previous year. By 2005, with consumer health care costs on the rise overall, CREST was looking for ways to control costs without cutting employee benefits. After looking at various options, I decided to branch off our training department into a separate entity, and the CREST Training Institute (CTI) was incorporated.

I stopped working directly for CREST, and instead became an employee of CTI, although I remained as president/CEO through a consulting agreement. This saved CREST many thousands of dollars in insurance costs and allowed me to share the training program I had developed with other companies in the industry.

My love for training was shared by a good friend and key member of the CREST team who had been with me from the start. Together, we formalized our program and began converting it to shareable media. We soon had production equipment, a filming room, editing capabilities, a full production studio, and additional personnel. We created a library of technical training and soft skills to teach technicians, from entry level all the way to experienced staff. We offered Continuing Education Units (CEUs), and were working toward college credits.

But as CREST continued growing, the time I could dedicate to CTI started to dwindle. More and more of my time was spent with CREST, which afforded the opportunity to grow and meet my long term goals. About two years into this venture, it became clear that CTI needed leadership and additional investment I couldn't provide without CREST suffering.

Unfortunately, the CTI chapter didn't end happily. The Institute closed, and the long-term friendship I had treasured ended. CREST continued using the CTI training materials for its employees for years afterward.

Enough time had passed and our employee count had increased to the point that our health insurance rates were not as affected by my past medical history, so I rejoined CREST as full time employee once again, with benefits.

CHAPTER 13

Truly a Family Business

Another big change was coming. The dealership group Brenda worked with had sold to new ownership, and the man she respected the most was retiring. Brenda had offered to come to help out at CREST, and I could see how her background in business financials was going to be a huge benefit to us.

At first I caught some reluctance from my management team on how someone from outside our industry could benefit us, and whether it was a good idea to bring a spouse into the company. I let her come in and earn her own way. It didn't take long before she became a go-to person within the organization. She earned the respect of both management and the field personnel. She was no longer "Brian's wife."

Have I mentioned that Brenda and I are complete opposites? I'm an extrovert, and she's an introvert. I love people, and she more closed. I'm a risk taker, and she's conservative. Being opposites isn't always easy, but if you can embrace the differences, it can be wonderful. We still had our challenges. One time, she actually resigned and was going to work elsewhere, so our differences would not interfere with our relationship. Of course as president/CEO, I declined to accept her resignation. In the end we balanced each other, which was a strength for our marriage and became a strength for the business.

At home, our conversations always seemed to circle back to the company, and even as we promised to take more time for ourselves and travel more, we naturally became more and more focused on business. We were committed though to not let work take us away from the family. We just knew the company was our future for security for the family. We were able to use it to our advantage as Brenda started taking business trips with me. We told ourselves that was one way to achieve our goal of traveling together more.

Under Pressure

Brenda and I truly believed our employees at CREST were family. Like family, they depended on us to continue growing the company to support them. My tendency to always want more also drove my desire to see the company grow so our family would be even bigger.

More growth meant more decisions and more stress, and the pressure of having so many people depending on me began to build. Pre-cancer, stress was never an issue. I always managed it well. Post-cancer, as I mentioned, I lost a few steps mentally. My memory faded a bit, my thought processes seemed slower, and my mind wasn't as sharp as it used to be. I tried to downplay it by likening my mind to a computer's aging RAM and processor speed. In all honesty, I became pretty concerned.

In 2005, I was officially diagnosed with "chemo brain," a common term used by cancer survivors to describe the thinking and memory problems that often occur after treatment. Chemo brain is also called "chemo fog," "chemotherapy-related cognitive impairment," or "cognitive dysfunction."

Whatever you call it, chemo brain means you forget things you usually have no trouble recalling. In addition to memory lapses, I began having trouble concentrating. I couldn't focus on what I was doing, I had a short attention span, and I often found myself spacing out. I also had trouble remembering details like names, dates, and sometimes details tied to more important events. I couldn't multitask. It took me longer to finish things because of slow and disorganized thought processes. I even had trouble remembering common words.

Ultimately, chemo brain made me start to question whether I should be leading the company.

Internal Struggles

Now that I was questioning whether I was the right person to take the company to the next level, I started wondering if I should sell CREST. I was only eighteen months post-transplant, and I wasn't back to my full health or energy. I expected the cancer to return any time, and I'd already decided I wasn't going through treatment again. We both figured we would deal with it when it happened. It had been the hardest, most unimaginable fight I had ever had and I just didn't feel I could do it again. It had had such a horrible effect on my body, but more importantly it had affected me as a person. At the end of the day, if it had returned I would have fought with all that I had. I could never have given up and Brenda would never have let me give up.

CREST had grown to the point that it was attracting industry attention, and bigger companies were calling with offers to buy. I was tempted to sell. CREST had grown beyond my ability to do what I felt I needed to do, and I wasn't sure I had the strength, energy, or even desire to continue growing the company.

Many people, including my most trusted advisors, told me that my job as CEO and president should be to set the direction of the company and put the right people in place to do the job. They told me I shouldn't be out in the field dealing with front-line employees and customers all the time. Instead, I should be in the corner office, setting strategy, giving direction, and "leading."

This didn't sound like the role for me — it didn't fit with my personality or definition of leadership. I could do strategy and set goals, I could lead teams and motivate employees, but if I wasn't supposed to interact with customers and employees on a daily basis, how could I be happy?

In 2005, for all these reasons, I decided to entertain an offer from one of the companies that had been calling whose philosophy seemed to match mine. Brenda wasn't fully on board with CREST yet in her role as financial controller, so I asked a trusted business advisor to accompany me to that meeting—it was a big decision and I wanted another perspective.

On the way back, my advisor showed me a graph he sketched on a napkin that described three basic options for growing a company after it reaches a certain size:

- Continue as is, in which case the company will eventually die without outside assistance.

- Hire outside professional management assistance to continue growth.

- Sell to outside investors and grow with their assistance.

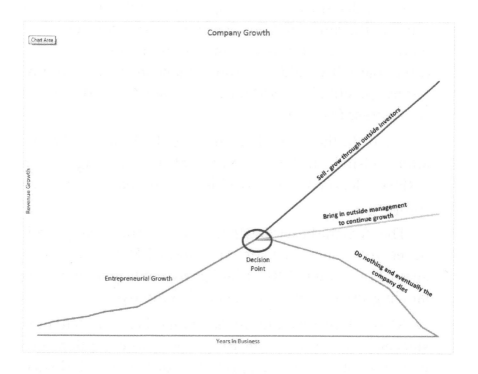

His point was that a company can only grow so far with an entrepreneurial spirit at the helm; at a certain point, a decision has to be made.

That graph was a major game changer for me, and I decided to sell.

I was convinced I didn't have the experience, knowledge, or education to move CREST past the $10 million mark. After all, we'd come out of 2003 and 2004 with no growth, and 2005 was going to be a critical year for CREST. We had invested so much for growth out of our cash flow and I had had to deal with my cancer. We were at a crucial stage for the company, having hit the fifty-employee mark.

In hindsight, I was letting others influence me too much at the time. I felt this was the best decision, one that would give our employees—and me—a more successful career path. It would give some financial cushion for my family, potential growth for my employees, and remove some stress from me.

What do they say about the best-laid plans? Shortly after a visit with the company that was offering to buy CREST, I learned they'd decided to purchase a different company.

That was the best thing that ever could have happened. Seven years later, that company and CREST would meet again, but by then, CREST had grown to fifty million dollars in gross revenue with over 250 employees.

Many decisions and goals change based on circumstances, and my decision to sell was no exception. We were one of the most respected leaders in our industry and attracting good talent. So with options one and three off the table, option two seemed like the way to go, and I hired outside help.

Consumed Again

When you're an entrepreneur, your business and your personal life often become one. By 2006, the company had become my life again, and now it also became Brenda's life. We were still determined we were not going to let the business get in the way of our personal life though. We were taking our family vacations and Brenda and I were taking ours. We had the added bonus of Brenda being able to travel with me on business trips. I wasn't missing Brice's orchestra concerts or Braden's baseball games.

Brenda had achieved a great grasp of what was happening in the company and industry as we traveled to customer sites and attended industry conferences together. She had taken full control over the business financials as the CREST controller. She knew every dollar we spent and could find a missing penny in a million dollars. She had established a fully staffed accounting department and was training them which allowed her to travel with me.

CREST became everything to us. It was all we talked about, all we did. It was our life, and the employees were like family.

CREST became more and more ingrained in us until we became synonymous with the company. Because of this, for the next six years, our personal story is also the story of CREST.

By 2007, revenue was up more than 50 percent and our net profit margin was over 15 percent. I'm not a "by the numbers" guy, but in business, you need metrics to determine whether you're succeeding and growing. Sometimes the numbers are the easiest tangible measurement of a company, but we still believed employee and customer satisfaction levels were just as important.

All the company's profits went back into the company, reflecting our "invest in our future" strategy. In 2008, we purchased a new building that would become our new corporate office, we invested in new technology, and we dedicated significant money to corporate overhead salaries. We also hired our first chief operating officer — someone who knew much more about corporate business than I did — to help guide our growth.

He was a successful businessman and understood the challenges of growing a business. He was also the advisor who had attended that prospective sales meeting with me as a favor in 2005 and had stayed on as an outside consultant. He had shown me that chart on the plane and helped me talk through the options. As soon as I knew I was going to bring in outside management, I asked him to come on full time. I needed his business acumen to take the next steps. Looking back, with more business experience under my belt, I could better understand what my boss from the other company had been trying to accomplish. Bringing in "outsiders" with more business knowledge and experience made more sense to me (but I still didn't agree with his method).

The year 2008 was a turning point. With the aging of baby boomers, the health care industry was primed for growth. Business was increasing substantially and opportunities continued to appear, but we needed to plan for continued expansion. We had invested so much in the company that we had no choice but to keep going. We now had over 100 employees across twenty states.

We focused on several key factors we hoped would lead to further success and refocused on our corporate vision and mission—to be the employer of choice. I believed if I treated my employees right, they in turn would provide unbelievable customer experiences, thus producing a healthy bottom line. There was a lot more to it than that, but "employer of choice" was the key phrase.

Develop your personal mission and then live by it. Check every decision against it.

I started working to engage the leadership of CREST to fully live our vision and mission, published new goals for the company, and continued building toward the future.

Brenda has never been the visionary of the family. She didn't buy in to why I was always talking about the vision and mission. Her philosophy was more along the lines of "they know their job; they just need to do it." This, in theory, is absolutely correct. In reality, it doesn't work that way.

I would always relate business principles to real life stories. Since I was now coaching Braden's baseball team, I used baseball as an example.

The baseball team's owners hire the general manager and coaches. The owner sets the direction of the team and decides where to invest in growth. The coaches and GM train and lead the players. The team moms provide the back office support. They help with scheduling games and coordinating practice and any team logistics. As for the players: if the catcher calls the right pitch, the pitcher pitches it great, the fielders' play their position, the batters hit the ball and run the bases, and if all of this is based on the right call from the coaches, without errors, you will win the game.

By 2009, CREST was truly focused on living the vision and mission of being the employer of choice, an industry leader competing at the highest level. Most importantly, we refocused our field personnel and management on service delivery and began developing specialized corporate support functions to allow the operational personnel to dedicate more time to customers and operations rather than financials and administrative support.

In mid-2009, these efforts were rewarded when we signed one of the biggest contracts in our industry, a ten-year, multi-million-dollar contract with a large health-care group. This group was concerned about the future of their long-term employees, so CREST committed to not only transition their people but to go above and beyond by protecting their status (position, salary, benefits, seniority); this commitment was a key factor in our being awarded the business.

For the rest of that year and throughout 2010, we focused on a seamless transition of more than one hundred employees along with the assumption of all assets and vendor agreements while merging best practices, data, policies, and procedures. It was a huge undertaking.

Managing 100 additional employees while attempting to maintain the same culture and company philosophies was a challenge, as was adding significantly more sophisticated equipment while merging two large service groups. Looking back, I'm extremely proud of the fact that we didn't lose a single employee that year.

As successful as we were in this regard, I was less successful at trying to balance my personal goals — spending more time with my family and not traveling for business as much — with company goals, including growth, focusing on employee relations, and customer service.

Up until this point, all of our leadership had been home grown, with the exception of our COO. I decided to bring in outside help to fill some of the higher-level positions.

Almost immediately, longtime employees began questioning why we needed the help of "outsiders." This was a problem, because seeing new leaders as "outsiders" limited the cohesiveness of the leadership team. I knew from experience that we would never have a *great* team with this type of divisiveness.

With everyone busy trying just to maintain, I went on the lookout for the additional staff we needed. I didn't need someone like me or the rest of my team. I needed someone who would complement our current structure and fill the gaps in expertise and experience. Most of my management staff, including me, had never worked for larger, corporate-type companies. I knew we couldn't continue running as a mom-and-pop company. We had to think bigger. Bring in new ideas. Not be so stuck in our current ways and be willing to step outside our current box.

Simultaneously, I realized that in order for the company to continue to grow and support new business, we would have to change or at least adapt to a larger-company mentality. Bringing in outside talent would help us learn how to have a larger-company mentality with new ideas to help us grow. However, these "outsiders" wouldn't necessarily have the same core values the CREST homegrown management team embodied. The challenge would be bringing them together as one and building mutual respect for the value each person brought to the team.

> *Surround yourself with people you can trust, and then learn to let go and let them handle things.*

Managing change became my focus, but I was adamant that we would maintain the core philosophies that had gotten us to where we were.

It was Brenda who stepped up first and said we needed a chief financial officer. She was right, and this individual needed to be someone we could trust. We made a call to an old friend Brenda knew and believed in. He accepted, and the position was filled.

My current chief operating officer knew nothing about our industry but he knew business—big business—and he taught me a lot about the business aspects of larger companies. He worked for CREST for about two years, but eventually I realized my COO needed to know more about our actual operations. We parted ways, and I started looking elsewhere to fill that role.

We needed a COO with experience in bigger companies, strong industry knowledge, and a personality and approach that was the opposite of mine. I was looking for someone to drive change—someone to be more business-focused than people-focused while still maintaining our people-first commitment.

I had talked to a few people and was recruiting some top names in the industry when the right person turned up. He had the experience and knowledge I needed, and was very much my opposite. The timing was right, so in 2010 I hired our first vice president of operations—from the outside.

I changed the position title from COO to the vice president role to give him room to grow. This was also some protection for me to make sure he could adapt to the philosophies I had instilled in CREST. I wasn't concerned with his industry experience or the fact that he was different from me. I needed him to earn the role of COO by gaining the respect of the employees and current leadership team.

Realizing I couldn't afford to take a big risk, and not wanting to put all my eggs in one basket, I also hired four other key support personnel. I had the opportunity to bring on some top talent to expand our strengths, and I was confident we were putting the right players in place to build a great team.

I knew that bringing in "outsiders" would present a number of challenges, but I must admit that it proved more difficult than I'd expected. The fact is, no one likes change forced upon them, even when it's for the good.

The basic problem centered around the question of *who* should change. Should it be the longtime CREST employees, the ones that had "always done it this way" that should change to fit the ideas of the "outsiders," or should the "outsiders" bend to CREST's way, even though it was radically different from what they knew?

I likened our situation to the infamous story about monkeys in a cage. In case you haven't heard it before, let me explain.

You start with a cage containing five monkeys. Inside the cage, you hang a banana on a string and place a set of stairs under it. Before long, a monkey will go to the stairs and start to climb toward the banana. As soon as he touches the stairs, you spray all the other monkeys with cold water. After a while, another monkey makes an attempt at the stairs with the same result—all the other monkeys get sprayed with cold water. Pretty soon, whenever a monkey starts to climb the stairs, the other monkeys try to stop him.

Now, put away the cold water. Remove one monkey from the cage and replace it with a new one. The new monkey sees the banana and wants to climb the stairs. To his surprise and horror, all the other monkeys attack him. After another attempt and attack, he knows that if he tries to climb the stairs, he will be assaulted.

Next, remove another of the original five monkeys and replace it with another new one. The newcomer goes to the stairs and is attacked. The previous newcomer takes part in the punishment with enthusiasm. Continue on, replacing a third original monkey with a new one, then a fourth, then the fifth.

Every time the newest monkey takes to the stairs, he is attacked. Most of the monkeys beating him up have no idea why they aren't permitted to climb the stairs or why they're participating in beating the newest monkey. All they know is that monkeys can't be on the stairs.

Once all the original monkeys have been replaced, even though none of the monkeys have ever been sprayed with cold water, no monkey ever approaches the stairs again to try for the banana for one simple reason: as far as they know, that's the way it's always been done.

As I mentioned earlier, change is not easy for some people to accept. Like the monkey story, CREST had done well and we had always "done it this way," so some questioned why we needed to change. Leadership is about growing business and people, while balancing the two.

If a company is going to grow and not die, it must always be changing to adapt to new and better ways of doing business.

As far as CREST was concerned, I figured that bringing in the best of the best would automatically make the company better. Everyone on my trusted staff would understand they were on our team for a reason, and they would respect the value each person brought for the mutual benefit of the company.

As I was to learn, bringing in senior executives from the outside would put this theory to the test. Bridging the gap between new and old employees and building a cohesive team of leaders to take CREST to the next level would, in fact, prove to be the most difficult challenge of my entire career.

CHAPTER 14

Applying What I'd Learned

Ever since its incorporation in 1999, I had insisted CREST adhere to two basic philosophies:

1. Engaged employees lead to satisfied customers and a financially sound company.

2. Our company will always "do the right thing."

I was determined to focus on believing in people, utilizing their strengths, and supplementing their weaknesses. Because the strengths of our operational personnel were technically oriented and customer focused, we developed a model of service delivery in the shape of a tripod. The tripod's three legs consisted of employees, customers, and vendors, and each leg of the model was fully dependent on the others. If one failed, the entire system failed.

> Apply what you've learned and what you believe in and watch what happens!

Employees were the primary pivot point. Customers were obviously necessary to maintain a successful and growing business, but we also recognized vendors as a key leg to our model since they supported our delivery of service. Developing vendor relationships to help us accomplish our goals became vital, and these relationships had to be true win-wins so the end result was highly satisfied customers. In turn, highly satisfied customers would become a "stepping-stone" to our growth.

Defining beliefs and values is critical to making the good decisions required to lead a business to success. Over time we identified formal corporate belief statements, all based on the following:

- Continued success is dependent upon our commitment to employees and their commitment to excellence.

- Focusing on employee satisfaction yields higher customer satisfaction, which leads to an increase in market share.

- Success is measured through continued growth and by exceeding customer expectations.

In 2011, we reestablished corporate goals with the understanding that in order to carry out our mission of having an "emphasis on deliverables, believing that good, well-informed decisions are the driving factor to success," we needed to focus on data-driven decisions.

"Good decisions will lead to a good bottom line" was actually written into our 2011 goals. Well-informed and educated personnel would make those good decisions, which required an emphasis on management/leadership training and performance management in the form of feedback to employees.

In 2012, we began measuring what we'd been working toward. We increased communication to all employees via monthly town hall meetings and focused on innovation. Our custom equipment management software package underwent a major upgrade, and we completed an in-depth review and analysis of all corporate processes, our organizational structure, job descriptions, administrative and operational policies and procedures, and service delivery strategies. Brenda had also taken the accounting team through a major transition during a conversion to a more advanced software package to handle the increased accounting requirements. This was done with an eye toward implementing the necessary changes in 2013 to align CREST for the next level of growth.

In 2012, Modern Healthcare named CREST Services one of the Top 20 outsourcing firms for the seventh year in a row. Our healthy profit margin and debt-free status validated that our unique style of business did indeed drive success. We had accomplished a successful employee oriented company using John Maxwell's theory of 360-degree leadership to drive a healthy financial bottom line.

In less than fourteen years, our organization had become a recognized, respected, well-branded name in our industry as an employee-oriented service company people wanted to be a part of because of our basic core philosophies.

My approach to business proved successful over and over, and I have many stories that show why putting others first results in success. Simply put, CREST didn't grow because of a big marketing and sales budget. We signed new business deals because we treated our customers right and they wanted to work with us because of it. How do we know this to be a true statement? Almost all our new business came from referrals. Meanwhile, employees wanted to work for us because of our reputation, which in turn enabled us to hire top talent.

Living the Vision

How did we live our vision to be the "employer of choice"? For starters, from the very beginning until 2008, when we became too big to coordinate the logistics, we hosted an annual holiday party for all employees and their spouses in Dallas. I always felt it was important to include spouses so they felt like part of the company, too.

Each party was different from the last, which made it exciting and created anticipation throughout the year. These parties included everything from comedy shows to magic shows to talent shows to casino nights to award banquets. And they were big — we pulled out all the stops to celebrate our people and their accomplishments for that year. Everything was about employee and spouse engagement, making them feel part of something special.

Once the company grew so large that we could no longer bring everyone in for a party, Brenda and I started traveling throughout the month of December to attend regional parties. This became a bit challenging personally, not to mention a logistical nightmare, so eventually I came up with a new way to engage employees. Soon, the infamous CRESTmas game became one of the first things new employees learned about from their peers.

This month-long game was designed to involve every employee and give them the opportunity to win prizes ranging from fifty dollars in cash to small electronics, iPads, and gaming systems.

I loved the game. Best of all, it allowed me to talk to employees three times a day for a month.

Toward the end of November, we would put out an announcement that the game was about to begin. Everyone was invited to send an email requesting their number. We created a game board with fifty spaces that showed the photo of support personnel or the nominees for the year's awards. Under each named block was a prize.

The board was posted online and when you viewed it and hovered over a block you would see more information about that person. This gave everyone a chance to learn more about other employees in the company.

The game would begin on December first and continue through Christmas Eve. Three times per day a number was drawn and emailed out to the entire company. The person who had the lucky number had fifteen minutes to call a special phone number to reach "Brian (Santa) Claus."

After chatting for a few minutes, I would ask for the name they selected on the board and I would reveal their prize. If they had not been paying attention and chose a name that had already been uncovered, they would lose their turn and their number would go back into the drawing.

Everywhere I went throughout the month of December, I saw CRESTmas game boards posted in shops and team members looking out for each other. More than once, a team member would call in for a technician who was deep in a repair and couldn't get away, or for someone who was on vacation.

Each year as the holidays approached, you'd start hearing chatter about when the game would start and what each team's strategy would be to ensure they were all covered if their number was drawn. It took time, energy, and money to run this game, but the rewards were tremendous. The teamwork that came out of it was invaluable, and the excitement and energy carried throughout the year.

I always tried keeping everyone engaged. The little things meant the most. We sent Thanksgiving cards out to every employee. Each card included fifty dollars to purchase a turkey. But that wasn't all. Two out of 250 cards would be signed differently. Maybe it would just say Brian instead of Brian Montgomery. Maybe Brian and Brenda had signed on opposite sides of the card. No one knew, but when we announced the difference a couple of weeks later, the employee who had that card (and could produce it) would win another $100 gift card.

To further engage our employees, we stepped up communication around what was happening corporately with live town hall presentations on the first Thursday of every month. For about an hour, I'd host a live webinar to update the entire company on what was going on.

We always personalized these presentations by recognizing birthdays, company anniversaries, new babies, college graduations, and more. We focused on one support department each month, and we also gave financial updates and operational and sales updates.

These town halls were actually suggested by an employee during a "CEO for the Day" contest we hosted annually. I asked employees to tell me what they would do if they were in my seat; the winner received a cash award and corporate recognition.

I loved reading all the submissions. They included everything from giving across-the-board pay raises to changing the tool kits we provided our technicians. A few ideas stood out, like holding the town halls, starting an internal marketing program, providing company-branded dress shirts, and making policy and procedural changes.

Mimicking the experience I'd had as a potential employee back in 1987 that led to me to move to East Texas in the first place, we also conducted prospective employee interviews differently than traditional job interviews. My goal was to get prospective employees excited about the company. By the time it was their turn to talk, they were desperately in love with the idea of becoming part of our team.

We held new employee orientations at the corporate office and brought every new employee to Dallas for a three-day orientation. They met every member of the support staff and learned about the company. I personally spent a lot of time with each group in order to infuse them with my passion and excitement. We treated these new employees like the most important people in the company, and I never looked at these events as an expense — they were a sound investment in the future of CREST.

During orientation, after welcoming the new employees and introducing the support staff, I spent a few hours telling our new employees about the history of CREST, our business philosophy, and my expectations. I also told my cancer story, as it's as much a part of CREST as it is my life. Some people don't believe a president and CEO should relate to employees on such a personal level, but telling stories and relating to people has always been how I do business.

The ultimate reward came one day when an employee called to request a personal meeting with me. He'd heard my cancer story during orientation and had recently been diagnosed with cancer himself. He wanted to bring his wife to meet me and let her hear my story.

We met, I offered words of encouragement, and we spent some time talking before I connected him with my oncologist and hospital. We became very close over the next few years, but he lost his battle with cancer in 2011. We named an award after him at our annual employee recognition banquet, and one of my most prized possessions is a statue his wife gave me after his death along with a letter he wrote to me before he passed away.

All of these efforts made people feel they were a part of something bigger than themselves. By personalizing CREST and engaging our employees, we also lowered turnover, which led to further company success.

There were costs—both time and money—but they were minimal compared to the loyalty, commitment, and dedication we received in return.

Entrepreneurial Challenges

An entrepreneur is basically someone who takes a risk on a business idea and builds on that idea.

I never thought of myself as an entrepreneur, but by definition, I guess I am. I was happy working for someone else as long as I believed in the company, but sometimes circumstances dictate a change, and change can be good.

Failure can be good, too. Most successful people fail many times before actually succeeding. Just look at Thomas Edison and the lightbulb. Failures highlight the lessons that allow us to learn and grow. The old adage, "It's not a mistake if you learn from it" is true. How you handle mistakes and failures is what defines you. Is there a failure or mistake in your life you've learned from?

In my lifetime, I've started four companies:

- First was my lawn cutting business as a teenager. That business supported my hobbies, paid for college, and led me to setting a goal of wearing a tie.

- Advantage Computers allowed me to use my passion to help people bring computers into their lives. Unfortunately, I wasn't able to make enough money to support my family full-time due to the changing computer industry and competition, so I closed this business.

- CREST Training Institute started as a way to save money on health insurance and ultimately closed due to a lack of leadership and time. One of our goals was to stream training videos online, but this technology was still in its infancy, and when we weighed all the options, the time and additional investment needed to continue developing it was simply too much.

- CREST Services was my success; it allowed me to fulfill my life goals.

Each of these businesses had a unique set of challenges. Every business does. I never saw the ongoing business challenges as a problem because I was doing what I loved. I took the challenges as part of the excitement, part of the game.

The personal challenges were another story. They were tougher for me to overcome. As is true for everyone who starts a company based on their beliefs and values, it became hard to maintain my core philosophy as more and more people were hired and given higher levels of responsibility. With increased business came a higher demand for financial reporting, increased human resources, and employee issues, along with increased stress on my personal life.

I needed to realize that what worked for a five million-dollar company might not work for a twenty-five-million-dollar company, and what worked for a twenty-five million-dollar company might not work for a fifty million-dollar company. People and processes had to be upgraded. As the entrepreneur, my role had to change as well. What it took to start the company and what it took to continue building it were two different things, and they constantly changed.

Maybe an example will help explain what I mean. If you're good at building widgets and you start a widget building company, you can handle the initial business. Once you start selling more widgets than you can build personally, you must hire someone else to help build them and train that person to build them the way you would. As the demand for widgets grows, you keep hiring more and more people. As you hire more people to build more widgets, you need more sales to keep the people you've hired employed. As more people are hired, someone has to pay them and handle employee issues. Meanwhile, the government wants its share of the widgets being sold, so someone has to handle the taxes. As the widgets become popular outside of your initial geographic location, other locations are needed to build those same widgets. You might even start looking at automation and technology to keep up with the demand or increase efficiency.

The demands and needs of the company continue to grow along with the company. This is true for any business as it moves from start-up into growth mode. Sometimes growth comes slowly and the business has time to adjust along the way. Other times, the growth comes fast and furious and internal struggles develop. Sometimes, the growth literally happens overnight. If you don't have the processes and people in place to support that growth, it can be incredibly challenging—even devastating.

As the growth happens, maintaining the culture you created becomes the greatest business challenge of all. As for me, this was one challenge I never anticipated.

Once entrepreneurs begin to grow their idea, they soon realize no one is going to do things exactly like they do—the way they treat people, the ownership they feel for the company, the passion they feel. The standards entrepreneurs set in their mind are higher than the average employee desires to deliver. Expecting all your employees to be as committed as you are is unrealistic.

Keeping Our Options Open

By late 2011, we were deep in the struggle of maintaining the culture we had built. Mutual respect among my senior leaders had all but disappeared, and the team I had built was neither cohesive nor working together. I desperately wanted my team to become *great*, but the idea of "doing the right thing" became muddled. Egos got in the way of the bigger purpose and goals, values were questioned, and financial performance was becoming a bigger focus. Not only was I questioning everything I had worked toward and stood for, but I also began to see the end of a great thing.

Keep your eyes and ears open. Think with your brain and listen to your heart.

I set the goals and direction of the company, but I couldn't get the executive team on the same page to implement them. I was trying to teach my management team to look at the bigger picture and not just their job. I needed them to appreciate the other members of the team and the value they each brought.

It was like my baseball analogy. If you are the pitcher, pitch and trust that the first baseman will catch the ball. If you play outfield, be ready when the ball comes to you. You have to be ready to do your job, you have to trust others to do theirs, and you all have to play the same game!

I had to decide whether to keep the leadership team I had built and try to force them into cohesiveness or to restructure the organization and let one or more of these people go. It was a decision that would put me back in the thick of things — a place I didn't want to return to.

I was caught between a rock and a hard place. I had already learned in my first management role that you couldn't force people to follow you just because you're the boss, but restructuring wasn't my preferred solution either. They clearly weren't following me, so was the problem my leadership?

When you encounter one or two challenges or are faced with reevaluating your values or priorities, the obstacles can be manageable. When you begin to question your own ability to lead, the challenge seems insurmountable. Hoping people will change or step into a role isn't enough.

It's a bit like raising kids. After you've done all you can do, it's up to them to take what they've learned and run with it. All you can do is trust that they'll use the values you've taught them when making decisions.

The problem at CREST was that I hired a great management team, but they weren't yet a great leadership team. No one person was ready to take the final step to bring the team together. Not even me.

Meanwhile, I was receiving letters and calls almost weekly from interested private equity firms and competitors, but money for the sake of money wasn't what I wanted or needed. I had no interest in selling the company just to infuse more dollars; what I wanted was for the company to grow and be great.

Right about this time, I received a call from an international firm looking to expand into the United States and simultaneously develop its international service lines.

Brenda and I were intrigued. After an initial meeting in Dallas, we flew to Europe to check out their operations and were presented with a proposal. Sure enough, their goals, our goals for CREST, and Brenda's and my personal goals were in alignment.

We made one additional trip to London to work out the details, and after a productive meeting, we decided to introduce the two companies. I believed this was the answer I'd been looking for, so I scheduled a visit for their team to meet ours.

One by one, Brenda and I spoke to the members of the management team to let them know about the upcoming meeting. We asked them to prepare a presentation for the meeting, explaining what their department did and why it was important in the big picture. As a team, we spent three days, working late into the night, preparing for the meeting.

To my utter amazement, my management team shined. Everyone worked together and truly respected each other as they worked toward the mutual goal of telling the CREST story to a prospective partner. I focused each one of them on their department. They only had a short period of time to sell their department's value. They had no time to worry about the others.

I grew prouder each and every time one of our leaders got up to talk about their department and how it served the vision, mission, values, and goals of our organization. We took their team out to visit some of our customers, and our employees and customers confirmed everything we said.

At long last, CREST was where I'd envisioned it. I could see this venture would ultimately allow us to grow into the fierce international competitor I knew we could become.

As we got closer to finalizing the deal, the European market began to decline. After many late night discussions, Brenda and I decided something wasn't right. On the Sunday prior to signing, I pulled the plug. Sometimes in business you have to go with your gut, and believe in yourself and the values you carry.

This turned out to be a great decision. Shortly thereafter, the European market crashed. The sale most likely would have defaulted anyway, and by pulling the plug when we did, we avoided a huge mess.

Nonetheless, the process confirmed we had a good thing going after all. Brenda and I were so proud that we decided to stay the course and continue to grow the company.

Continuing to Adjust and Learn

I learned a lot about big business from the process of preparing to sell CREST. I learned things like what due diligence means and what is required of a company being acquired. As a result, I gave in to implementing more financial controls and formal reporting.

I had never truly focused on budgets before—I'd always focused on making the right decisions and letting the bottom line take care of itself. The people we brought in from the outside were accustomed to focusing on the financials. They often told me that one of the attractive things about working for CREST was getting away from the financial focus, but old habits die hard.

After a short time, several employees started pushing for a more financially driven approach. After seeing what would be expected in an acquisition, and knowing that we'd one day need to position the company to sell, I gave in to their desire to develop and report against budgets.

Yet even as I continued to adjust and learn, I expected my people to do the same. More than anything, I needed them to embrace the same values and philosophies I did. I believed that promoting from within offered CREST the best chance of continuing to run the way I envisioned it, so I constantly evaluated key people to see who could handle the senior positions I needed filled. I believed the best form of motivation and reward was increased responsibility, and my goal was to identify those who could rise to the top.

Reminiscent of my grass-cutting days, I moved key employees around to different positions in order to expose them to as many different aspects of the company as possible. Some embraced this, but others never fully understood what I was doing.

Those who embraced the challenge advanced, but it didn't always work. I learned early on the downside of promoting people too soon. I lost good people during the grooming process because they wanted to advance quicker than I thought they were ready to, and I lost others who advanced but proved unable to handle it. It takes time to grow leaders from within, and in light of CREST's ongoing explosive growth, that presented a big challenge. We had many success stories, but some people did leave for various reasons. I'm proud to say that more than a few of these people became successful in other companies, and I hope I played at least a small part in that success.

Seeing the management team pull together to put CREST's best face forward when meeting the international team gave me hope that things would stay better, but they didn't. Maybe it was the fact that my people now knew I might actually sell the company, something my long-term employees had never expected, but whatever the reason, the camaraderie didn't last.

Instead, the daily grind returned, along with my frustrations with the management staff. Dealing with competing egos, attitudes of entitlement, and the different directions being exerted on our vision and mission took a big bite out of my enthusiasm. Once again, my leadership team was failing to exhibit mutual respect or to work together, and this called my abilities as a leader and motivator into question. How could I be an effective leader if I couldn't get my most senior leadership team on the same page?

All the while, I continued receiving advice from people I respected on how to run the business, who should be in charge, what I should be doing, and what I should *not* be doing.

The thing was, I didn't want to sit in my office all the time. I wanted to be out in the field, talking to people, engaging with employees and customers. So in order to regain my passion and enthusiasm, I started visiting client locations again to see our employees.

Ironically, I came to believe that this was what my management team *didn't* want—if I was out in the field, I might overshadow them and build stronger relationships with their people than they'd built. This was never my intent, but my personality encouraged this. I was actually hoping they would follow my lead and get out with their people more.

Consequently, I couldn't help but question anew whether a company the size of CREST could continue to operate under my leadership.

I had never really thought of it in a business frame of reference, but I see now I was looking for an exit strategy. I needed a way for the company to continue to exist without me. If the company was going to grow and I was going to be able to meet my long-term goal, I needed a plan.

The first step to developing that plan was to see where we truly were, not what I was hearing from the management team, but actually seeing and hearing what was going on across the company for myself. What happened turned out to be more emotional and dramatic than I expected, but it accomplished that objective.

The Results Are In

To my surprise, what I discovered when I began visiting my employees in the field was disheartening—not everyone was as happy as my management team had led me to believe.

Although we were clearly recognized as an industry leader and remained a good company to work for, CREST no longer met my personal goal of being what our mission statement said we were: "employer of choice."

I sent out an independent employee satisfaction survey to validate my concerns. The results made it clear that we were no longer a top company to work for, even though the employee comments would have given me a big head in my younger days. After all, they included statements such as:

- Brian is a great leader.
- We love working for Brian.
- Brian has a great vision for the company, but there's no one to carry it out.

Therein lay the problem. I was trying to build a company that was not "all about Brian," but "all about Brian" was exactly what I read over and over in those survey results. Even though the results of the survey were actually quite good and many companies and leaders would have loved them, it wasn't what I wanted to see and it wasn't where the company needed to be.

Sometimes you have to put your ego aside and focus on the greater good.

Don't misunderstand me—on paper, the company was doing great. But I was looking at the future of our company as well as at my fiftieth birthday coming up in three short years. My goal was to semi-retire at age fifty and begin enjoying life more. I didn't need my employees focusing on or believing in me; I needed them trusting and believing in my leadership team.

I came up with a drastic plan to elicit the thoughts of my leadership team and determine whether they could figure out a way to work together. This group included about fifteen people made up of both "outsiders" and homegrown CREST leadership. This is important to note because the team was still clearly made up of two distinct groups. Some were based in the corporate office and some were based in Dallas or at various locations across the country.

The night before our next regularly scheduled meeting, I pushed my big black executive desk chair behind a divider in the conference room.

When the meeting kicked off, the room was packed. The entire team was present. Most of them always chose the same seats in our meetings. Brenda was at her normal seat to my right. My assistant was to my left ready to take notes and run the presentation. Normally there was an agenda on the screen and on the table in front of them. This meeting was different.

I had run through this meeting in my head over and over during my sleepless night before. No one, including Brenda, knew what I was about to say. I'm not sure I even knew. I welcomed everyone and then simply asked if they'd read the survey results. I don't remember exactly what I said because when I get emotional, I tend to go off-script, but I do remember the answers I heard, and they weren't what I was looking for.

They thought the results were great. No one saw the problem.

I seldom get mad, much less furious, but this time, I'd reached my limit. My people weren't all on the same page, much less on the same page as me. I pulled my chair from behind the divider and told them to put themselves in it. What would they do with these results if they were me? I told them to come up with a solution and left.

I'm told there was a long period of awkward silence. That the tension was palpable. I'm still not sure to this day what was said in my absence, but I heard things got pretty intense.

As for me, I did what I always do when I need time to get away and think—I went to Costco to walk the aisles. I called Brice after I left Costco just to chat. He interned at CREST for a few years during college break and knew most of the management team. I could talk to him as a distant observer and take a step back from the situation.

I don't know what I was expecting upon my return, but I sure didn't get it. I guess I hoped they would figure out how to work together as a team, but that didn't happen. The solution I was presented with was to create an even more exclusive executive group, adding another level of management (made up entirely of outsiders) and essentially demoting the homegrown management staff. This would only divide the team further and was exactly what I didn't want to hear. I dismissed the meeting and made a phone call.

The company I'd almost sold CREST to seven years earlier had reappeared and was courting me pretty hard. Initially, I'd said selling CREST wasn't an option, but now I had changed my mind. It was time to implement option three — sell to outside investors and grow with their assistance.

This was one of the toughest decisions I'd ever made. I felt like I was letting many people down, but at the end of the day, it was time to make the best decision for myself, for my family, and for the company.

Personally, I couldn't continue down this same path. My health was declining due to stress, not from the cancer treatments. My blood pressure had climbed to the point that I'd begun taking medication, I couldn't sleep, and I was showing signs of depression. Once again, I was losing my passion and excitement.

People always energized and excited me, but now they drained and exhausted me. I was ready for a break from everyone. Brenda was no better. Her stress level was through the roof, so that helped finalize my decision.

After a lot of discussion, Brenda and I made the choice to sell. Happily, the acquiring company was employee-oriented. They planned to maintain CREST's support systems, merge the best practices from both companies, and utilize our infrastructure, since it was more advanced. Most importantly, this merger would offer our employees a better growth path. Both companies saw this as an opportunity to dominate the industry and make for a much stronger, better company in the end.

Brenda and I set some pretty unrealistic terms for the acquisition process. No one would be part of the due diligence process except our attorney. We would not introduce anyone from the new company to our people at CREST. We didn't dare—we feared we might back out. The fact that they agreed to our terms and gave tenure to all our employees made us feel confident that this was the right decision.

We made the announcement on December 20, 2012. That morning, we woke up knowing this would be an emotional day. We felt excitement and regret, happiness and sadness. We even joked about how working with the company and our employees had been like raising kids. They'd started out as babies, grown through their teenage years, and gone off to college. To finish the analogy, today was their wedding day. We felt like we were sending them off on their new lives, trusting we had been a sufficiently positive influence to help them be successful. We just hoped the two families were a good match and that everyone got along with the in-laws.

Not surprisingly, after our announcement, we were both congratulated and sneered at, hugged and cursed.

After a difficult day, we met our sons at Chili's for dinner and went to bed looking forward to getting up the next morning and going back to work.

Brenda and I had not talked about our personal future much other than taking a short break to continue marking off our bucket list. I agreed to stay on as president of CREST for three years to assist with the transition. There was to be a year of merging the best practices of both companies, which would create an unstoppable force in our industry. Brenda also agreed to stay on for one year to ensure a smooth transition of the financials — payables, receivables, and answering all the little questions that would inevitably come up. We had no set plans. We just needed a break. This would allow us to stay involved but relieve the tremendous stress we were both experiencing.

We were excited for the company. This was the opportunity we had looked for to compete on a higher level. Merging all the support systems we had built with another force that had financial backing was going to be incredible. Everything we had worked for, had dreamed about, had literally given blood, sweat and tears for, was coming to fruition.

CHAPTER 15

Life Goes On

Brenda and I have always tried to please and care for others, and for the most part, I think we've made a success of it. Someone once told me he'd never met two people who cared so much for others, one who wore it on his sleeve, and the other who refused to let you see it.

Brenda is a more closed personality type than I am; she doesn't easily let her guard down or show how she feels, but she loved our company and our employees every bit as much as I did. She was the first to step up and support adding benefits or implementing an extra program that would add to the employee experience. The employees were her family, too. Even though she's a more private person than I am, she cared deeply about the people and wanted to do the best we could for them.

With the sale of CREST in December 2012, part one of our story came to a close. I've turned fifty since writing this book and am living proof that doctors don't always know what's going to happen. I feel better than I've ever felt in my life, and I'm in better shape than I've been in years. I still felt some effects of the treatment and the chemo brain: sometimes my memory and mental sharpness aren't what I'd like them to be. I'm not as quick-witted as I used to be. Stress seems to get to me more easily than before.

Today, Brenda and I are enjoying part two of our story. We continue to check off items on our bucket list, and somehow we keep adding to it as we go.

Brice graduated with a mechanical engineering degree from Texas A&M University in 2013. Braden will begin his college career at Texas A&M in 2016, pursuing an engineering technology degree with a focus on automotive engineering.

When I speak about success today, I always begin with "I consider myself a successful person" and it's true:

- I married my childhood sweetheart and we are still married today – success.
- I have two awesome sons who have grown into amazing young men – success.
- I have been able to send them (and others) to college to assist in their future – success.
- I drive a Tesla (this seems to be everyone's favorite on the list!) – success.
- Brenda and I have been able to travel and meet new people – success.

We have built our beach home—the one that we dreamed of since that first trip to Jamaica when we felt the sun, put our toes in the in the sand, and enjoyed the sounds of the sea. We now enjoy waking up in the morning and seeing the sunrise with a cup of Belizean coffee as we stand in the backyard of our beach home, Casa Sunsandsea.

We shared a vision and lived it, and today we feel blessed to enjoy the fruits of all we accomplished. I still think about that question: Why am I here? But now I have a pretty clear answer.

Not bad for two country folks with little education and no money.

Looking Back, Looking Ahead

I don't think I ever imagined while growing up in small town Mississippi that I would be where I am today. I'm a goal-oriented person, but I always changed my goals to obtain more. Even when driving home to Mississippi in my early years of field service, I broke the trip into seventy- or one hundred-mile segments to support my long-term goal of getting home. These chunks were small enough to reach but large enough to make a difference.

I also changed my long-term goals a few times after exceeding my short-term ones, but I always kept in mind my ultimate goal of retiring early with little or no financial stress and being able to provide my family with the resources to have successful lives of their own.

The simple fact is, I always wanted more, and this was the driving force behind the risks I took. More risk equals more reward. Wanting more and being willing to risk what I had led to my success, but it's interesting to note that later in life, when I saw financial success was in

> *What's in your future? There will always be another story to tell, another book to write.*

my near future, my willingness to take risks dropped. I took fewer chances and became more conservative. Maybe it's easier to take chances when you have nothing to lose.

The advice I give people who run their own companies is to always listen to others, but don't always do what they advise. Consider their advice, but remember who had what it took to step off the ledge. Your spirit, your passion, and your gut made your success, so don't let those who never did it detour you.

Even though I made that mistake a few times, most of the decisions I made to grow CREST were gut decisions that came out of my character. Sometimes those decisions couldn't be easily explained, but the outcome cannot be denied.

Three years after selling the company that started in my house in 1999 and grew to over 250 employees and exceeded fifty million dollars in revenue, I have no regrets. I've lived my life by making decisions and taking responsibility for them, knowing I can do nothing about the past except learn from it.

It is nice to look back and reflect on your experiences. Not that you can change them, but you can learn more from them. We are always circling back to Principle 1 and learning something new.

We continue to focus on loving it—appreciating people and experiences in life. I am grateful that I was eventually able to reconnect with my mentor, the man I spent so much of my early career with. We now have regular lunch meetings just to talk and share experiences.

We are living it — life doesn't end when you meet your goal, when you find success. We have new experiences and new challenges. But we keep on living.

And we're pursuing it — meeting one level of success only leads to setting new goals. We're checking things off the bucket list, pursuing new business interests, and helping other people find their success.

Sure, I'd change a few things if I could, but one thing in life I've learned is that while every decision is critical, deciding how to treat people is the most important decision of all. I've always believed that making the right decisions is key to success and you make those decisions based on your character.

Nonetheless, sometimes I do look back at my life and wonder "What if?"

What if I'd fallen into the trap of not going to college? What if I'd taken the oil field job in East Texas because it would have paid more? What if that nurse had not encouraged me to interview? What if I'd decided to stay in Mississippi and not move to Texas? What if I hadn't discovered Brenda's heart problem? What if I'd decided not to work extra hours? What if I hadn't taken the chance to start a business? What if I'd given up on my marriage? What if I hadn't gone to the doctor?

It's easy to look back and wonder, but "it is what it is," as Brenda's favorite saying goes. We make the decisions, but we also get to live with them. That's why it's so critical to know now what you knew then.

I credit the CEO of the company where I spent most of my early career with putting me in situations that were outside my comfort zone and definitely beyond my job description. He sometimes pushed me past what seemed like my limits, but he always found a way to compensate me. Most of the time it was something small, that cost him little.

Likewise, I remember vividly how, on our wedding day, one of my old customers shook my hand with a $100 bill tucked in his palm. He told me to put that money in the back of my billfold, to only use it in an emergency, and to always replace it.

That experience had an impact on me, and I've often repeated it with other people. The fact is, many of my experiences had value beyond the paycheck and helped build my character.

Ultimately, success is achieved by remembering how you got to where you are. This is where loyalty comes into play. All the events that occur in your life make you who you are. That's why it's important to know now what you knew then.

The four basic principles that I have lived by and presented to you have proven successful for me.

I learned everything I could learn through experiences.

I had the love and passion for what I did. If you were counting, passion is mentioned over forty times throughout this book.

I believed in what I did and lived it despite many challenges and opportunities.

I pursued my goals with everything I had.

Most importantly, I remembered the feelings of both successes and failures with all their accompanying emotions, and used those feelings to drive everything I did.

Meanwhile, the lessons I learned as a young man continue to impact my life for the better today, and as I look ahead to tomorrow with Brenda by my side.

RESOURCES

- *See You at the Top* by Zig Ziglar
- *One Minute Manager* by Ken Blanchard
- *The 7 Habits of Highly Effective People* by Stephen Covey
- *The 360° Leader* by John Maxwell
- *Who Moved My Cheese?* by Spencer Johnson
- *How to Win Friends and Influence People* by Dale Carnegie

ABOUT THE AUTHOR

Brian Montgomery grew up in southern Mississippi where he learned at an early age about the value of leadership and the importance of extending compassion and respect to all people.

Born in July, Brian embraces the characteristics of a Leo and has developed a leadership style that centers on people. From his love of lions (evident from his collection of more than fifty paintings and statues, including a giant rendering carved from a tree stump) to the passion he displays in business and in life, his main focus is to use his strength to serve the many deserving people around him and beyond.

As an entrepreneur, his leadership style allowed him to build a multimillion-dollar business. Brian has faced many challenges along the way, including fighting late stage four cancer, and is most proud to call himself a cancer survivor.

Today, Brian enjoys life with his wife and family while helping others strive for success, whatever that may be for them.

In an effort to help budding business owners and entrepreneurs who need more hours in the day, Brian has created PrideGroupCo to supply executive virtual assistants to those needing an affordable administrative support system. You can learn more about them here: http://pridegroupco.com

He also enjoys speaking to groups of all sizes about his experience in life and in business. You can learn more about having Brian speak to your group here: http://theniceentrepreneur.com

Brian and Brenda enjoy spending time in their dream home on the beaches of Belize. See how it all came together at http://casasunsandsea.com